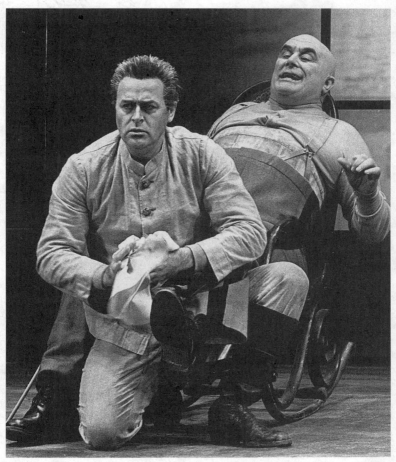

José van Dam (Wozzeck) and Hermann Winkler (Captain), Covent Garden, 1984 (photo: Clive Barda)

This Opera Guide is sponsored by

Wozzeck

Alban Berg

Opera Guide Series Editor: Nicholas John

John Calder · London
Riverrun Press · New York

Published in association with English National Opera

COPYRIGHT DATA

First published in Great Britain, 1990, by
John Calder (Publishers) Ltd,
9-15 Neal Street, London WC2H 9TU

First published in the USA, 1990, by
Riverrun Press Inc., 1170 Broadway,
New York, NY 10001

BRITISH LIBRARY CATALOGUING IN PUBLICATION DATA
Berg, Alban *1885-1935*
    Wozzeck.—(Opera guide series, 42).
    1. Opera in German. Berg, Alban, 1885-1935
    I. Title   II. Series
    780.92

    ISBN 0-7145-4201-6

LIBRARY OF CONGRESS CATALOGING NUMBER 90-44450

LIBRARY OF CONGRESS CATALOGING IN PUBLICATION DATA *is also available*

English National Opera receives financial assistance from the Arts Council of Great
Britain.

Typeset in Plantin by Maggie Spooner Typesetting, London NW5
Printed in Great Britain by The Southampton Book Co., Southampton

CONTENTS

Page

vi   List of Illustrations

7   'Wozzeck' in Context *Mark DeVoto*

15   Georg Büchner's 'Woyzeck': an Interpretation *Kenneth Segar*

23   The Musico-Dramatic Structure of 'Wozzeck'

25   Musical Form and Dramatic Expression in 'Wozzeck'
     Theo Hirsbrunner

37   On the Characteristics of 'Wozzeck' *Theodor W. Adorno*

41   'Wozzeck' at Covent Garden, 1952 *John Amis, Eric
     Walter White, Arthur Jacobs, William Mann, Joan Chissell,
     Geoffrey Bush, Deryck Cooke, Robert L. Jacobs*

53   Thematic Guide

57   'Woyzeck' *Georg Büchner, edited by Franzos and Landau, 1909*
     'Wozzeck' *performing translation of Berg's libretto by Vida
     Harford and Eric Blackall*
     Additional material from Büchner *translated by
     Stewart Spencer*

58   A comparative structure of the play and the opera

61   Act One

81   Act Two

100   Act Three

111   Discography *David Nice*

112   Bibliography, Contributors and Acknowledgements

LIST OF ILLUSTRATIONS

Cover design by Anita Boyd
Frontispiece: José van Dam and Hermann Winkler, Covent Garden, 1984

Page
9 Set design by Panos Aravantinos for the world première, Berlin, 1925
10 The first production in Darmstadt, 1931
11 The first production in Frankfurt, 1931
13 Set design by Robert Edmund Jones for the US première, Philadelphia, 1931
14 One of the sets of the first production in Prague, 1926
16 Scene from the 1942 Rome production
19 Walter Berry as Wozzeck, Vienna, 1955
21 Walter Berry as Wozzeck, Vienna, 1955
22 Hermann Uhde and Paul Franke in the Metropolitan Opera première, 1959
24 Karl Dönch and Hermann Uhde, Metropolitan Opera, 1959
26 Geraint Evans as Wozzeck, Covent Garden, 1960
32 Christa Ludwig as Marie, Vienna, 1963
34 William Dooley and Donald Gramm, Metropolitan Opera, 1965
36 Christel Goltz and Thorsteinn Hannesson, Covent Garden, 1952
43 Marko Rothmüller and Christel Goltz, Covent Garden, 1952
45 Frederick Dalberg and Marko Rothmüller, Covent Garden 1952
47 Frederick Dalberg, Marko Rothmüller and Parry Jones, Covent Garden, 1952
49 Christel Goltz as Marie, Covent Garden, 1952
50 David Tree and Jess Walters, Covent Garden, 1952
52 Christel Goltz and Marko Rothmüller, Covent Garden, 1952
55 Evelyne Lear as Marie, San Francisco Opera, 1968
56 Metropolitan Opera sets designed by Caspar Neher
65 Bodo Schwanbeck and Richard van Vrooman, Zurich, 1968
70 Above: Benjamin Luxon and Roderick Kennedy, Scottish Opera, 1983. Below: Donald McIntyre as the Doctor, Covent Garden, 1984
71 Above: Jürgen Freier as Wozzeck, Leipzig, 1985. Below: 'Wozzeck', Welsh National Opera, 1986
78 Anja Silja and James King, Covent Garden, 1984
97 Above: Hermann Winkler and Walter Berry, Cologne, 1975. Below: William Lewis and Benjamin Luxon, Scottish Opera, 1983
101 Hildegard Behrens as Marie, Metropolitan Opera, 1989

Picture research: Jennifer Batchelor

'Wozzeck' in Context

Mark DeVoto

For four years after the Great War broke out in August 1914, composers, like everyone else, were affected by rapidly developing events. As empires collapsed and new orders arose all over Europe, so did new musical languages and styles, aesthetic movements, and personal destinies. Igor Stravinsky, only a few weeks before the shooting began, had enjoyed the spectacular première of his opera *The Nightingale* and, as his neoclassical language formed in the next three years, he would not write a work as chromatic or as complex in texture for four decades. Béla Bartók would begin his longest orchestral work, the ballet *The Wooden Prince*, in 1914, finishing it two years later. Arnold Schönberg in 1914 was grappling simultaneously with the most difficult problems of musical form and personal theology in a huge symphony, which would be overshadowed by his oratorio *Die Jakobsleiter*; it would have been his largest and longest work, but it remained unfinished, a casualty of the war, and not until the 1920s would a new technique emerge in new works. Claude Debussy, for a decade the most illustrious composer in western Europe, was severely ill, and depressed by the suffering of his country; not until 1915 would he begin to write music again, in one final burst of creativity before his early death. Younger than any of these was Alban Berg, whose experience of the war helped him work out the musical expression of a debased human condition in his opera *Wozzeck*, a work which, nearly seventy years after its first performance, must still be considered the most remarkable opera of the twentieth century. *(Berg – 1885 – 1935)*

Berg had begun his studies with Arnold Schönberg in 1904 at the age of nineteen. Aside from a few elementary piano lessons, this was Berg's first formal instruction in music, and his extraordinary development in the next seven years, exclusively under Schönberg's guidance, is unique in the history of musical pedagogy. Beginning as a musically naive and inexperienced adolescent, Berg emerged in 1911 as one of the most mature composers of his time. This transformation came about as a result of both Berg's natural talent and Schönberg's great skills as a teacher; but just as important was Berg's opportunity to witness and to share in the environment of Schönberg's own intensive growth and development as a composer. Berg's works of these apprentice years include what he later called Seven Early Songs, songs in a late tonal idiom of great lyric and expressive intensity as well as formal mastery; the Piano Sonata, Opus 1, of 1908, which in its dense harmony and complex formal design, is clearly influenced by Schönberg's Chamber Symphony, Opus 9, of 1907; and the even more chromatic Four Songs, Opus 2, of 1909, in the last of which Berg experimented with atonal harmony for the first time. Berg's String Quartet, Opus 3 (1911), shows all of the Schönbergian lessons of thematic compression and development worked out in chromatic (and still partial tonal) contrapuntal texture of great power and conviction — the last work he was to write directly under Schönberg's supervision before the latter moved to Berlin.

The next three years marked Berg's first full independence before the Great War. Fresh from the première performance of Mahler's *Das Lied von der Erde* (November 1911), Berg began writing his first orchestral work, completed in 1912 under the title of *Five Orchestral Songs on Picture-Postcard Texts of Peter Altenberg*, Opus 4. To Berg's dismay, it failed to please Schönberg, and the first partial performance, on March 31, 1913, in Vienna, touched off a scandal which was reported all over Europe; these unpleasant circumstances caused Berg to put the songs on the shelf, denying one of his best works to the world for several decades. Neither did Schönberg much like Berg's next composition, the short Four Pieces for clarinet and piano, Opus 5, urging him instead to write longer and more developed works. The result was Berg's Three Pieces for Orchestra, Opus 6, begun in the spring of 1914 and completed during the summer of 1915. The beginning of Berg's intensive effort on the Three Pieces coincided with his attendance at an historic performance —the Vienna stage première of Georg Büchner's play *Woyzeck* with Albert Steinrück in the title role.

The author of *Woyzeck*, Georg Büchner, a native of Darmstadt, had been a medical student in Zurich before his death in 1837 at the age of twenty-three. He left to posterity only a small corpus of works, but enough to convince later generations of his literary genius. Among his works are a novella, a play about the French Revolution, *Danton's Death*, a comedy, *Leonce and Lena*, various socialist tracts which made him a fugitive from the Hessian authorities and, among his unpublished manuscripts and fragments, various drafts of a play, *Woyzeck*. The difference in spelling the title role is due to a misreading by the first editor of the play, Karl Emil von Franzos, who published it in 1879; Büchner's manuscript was so poorly legible that even today scholars disagree on many readings of the text. The structural problem is complicated by the lack of page numbers or scene numbers in the manuscript, and by the presence of many revisions of different scenes. Berg saw and used an edition by Landau, published in 1909, of Franzos's reading of Büchner.

It must have been immediately apparent to those who read Franzos's edition of *Woyzeck* that the play would be a controversial work to stage. That the dialogue is filled with slang and indecent expressions was the least of the problems. It was Büchner's dramatic conception which was so radical — the large number of scenes barely connected or completely unconnected by any narrative continuity, many of them extremely short; the disordered, often dreamlike, soliloquizing in fragmentary sentences; the intense and rapid pace of the thought process. Today we recognize all of these as characteristics of cinematography, with stream-of-consciousness narration, flashbacks, and rapid cutting from scene to scene and from viewpoint to viewpoint. Beyond this is Büchner's uncanny vision of an oppressive world populated by irrational and predatory people, in which only the simple soldier Wozzeck and his faithless wife Marie stand out with a measure of human sanity.

Regardless of the edition used, *Woyzeck*, the correct name of the protagonist now long since restored, has been a permanent part of the twentieth-century stage repertory and it has been recognized as one of the milestones in the history of literary and dramatic art. As the critic George Steiner has written,

> *Woyzeck* is the first real tragedy of low life. It repudiates an assumption implicit in Greek, Elizabethan, and neo-classic drama: the assumption that tragic suffering is the sombre privilege of those who are in high places.

Nor do we need to be reminded how depressingly authentic the subject sounds in our own century of violence and dehumanization.

We do not know much about what particularly musical reasons attracted Berg to the play. But the documentary basis is intriguing. In Berg's notebooks can be found a tabular layout of short scenes, side by side with a comparable layout of scenes for Debussy's opera *Pelléas and Mélisande*, a work about as different from *Wozzeck* as could be imagined but which shares with it one

Set design by Panos Aravantines for the world première at the Staatsoper, Berlin, 1925 (photo: Archiv Universal Edition)

important characteristic — the break-up of each Act into short scenes separated by orchestral interludes while the curtain is lowered. (The structure of Debussy's opera had been regarded as radical in its day, and he too had chosen a pre-existing stage play, by Maurice Maeterlinck, as the basis of his libretto.) Beyond this, we have the testimony of Berg's student Gottfried Kassowitz, who states that Berg began sketching two scenes for the music right after seeing the play — in other words, while he was working on the March in the Three Pieces for Orchestra, Opus 6; this is borne out by one of Berg's sketchbooks containing fifty pages of sketches for the March, and a number of miscellaneous sketches for the Fantasy in Act Two, scene two (the Captain and the Doctor) and for Act One, scene two (Wozzeck and Andres), as well as Berg's verbal notes about the kinds of characters he envisioned for his opera. Thus it is not at all surprising that part of the music which was ultimately included in Act One, scene two (bars 274-278) is derived from bars 81-90 of the March, which he was working on in the spring of 1914.

The surviving sketches seem to be in the form of musical ideas, quickly jotted down — short melodic or rhythmic fragments associated with specific lines of text, a few rudimentary harmonies that could have originated from experimenting at the piano, and an occasional bit of a more concentrated or worked-out texture. What is most striking about Berg's manner of sketching, as seen in the *Wozzeck* sketches and in earlier works, is his habit of writing down first a generalized rhythmic and melodic shape, a contoured line of stems and beams sprawled over the staff, without notes. In other words, Berg's choice of pitches is not an initial but an intermediate stage of composition, not decided until the writing of the short score, itself the last stage before the full orchestral score.

9

Berg's first task, in the summer of 1914, was to finish the Three Pieces, which he intended to dedicate to Schönberg. The Präludium and March were completed in time for Schönberg's birthday on September 13 but the second piece, *Reigen*, was not finished until the summer of 1915. And on August 15, 1915, Berg reported for infantry training; two months later he was sent to a reserve officers' school at Bruck-an-der-Leitha in what is now Hungary.

Berg's experience as a soldier, even without seeing combat, was no different from that of millions of others. 'From seven in the morning till one in the afternoon we were marching, running, charging across hill and dale, through the swamps and marshes, down to the ground, up again, and so on', he wrote to his wife. 'I've got a crust of mud all over me. Afternoon out again, but at least without pack or rifle.' He once remarked to Kassowitz, 'Have you ever heard a lot of people all snoring at the same time? The polyphonic breathing, gasping and groaning makes the strangest chorus I have ever heard.' He remembered this when he wrote the snoring chorus in Act Two, scene five of *Wozzeck*. His physical constitution, however, was not up to much rough activity, and in November, following an aggravation of his bronchial asthma, he was reassigned to guard duty in Vienna, and eventually to a job in the War Ministry, where he remained till the end of the war. In 1919, defending his 'fierce antimilitarism' in a letter to his pupil Erwin Schulhoff, he recalled his time in the War Ministry: 'Two and a half YEARS of *daily* duty from eight

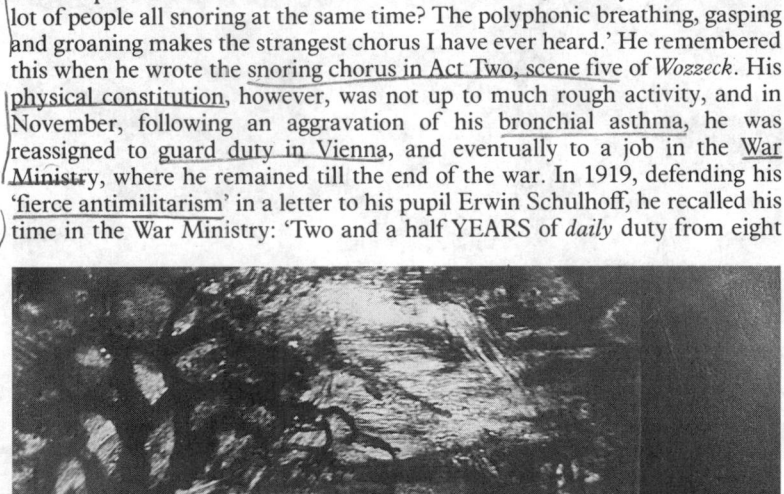

The first production in Darmstadt, 1931, conducted by Karl Böhm, with Albert Lohmann (Wozzeck) and Johannes Schocke (Andres); producer, Renato Mordo, designer, Lothar Schenck von Trapp (photo: Archiv Universal Edition)

The first production in Frankfurt, 1931, with Jean Stern (Wozzeck) and Erna Recka (Marie); producer, Herbert Graf, designer, Ludwig Sievert (photo: Archiv Universal Edition)

o'clock in the morning to six or seven in the evening of onerous paperwork under a frightful superior (a drunken imbecile!). All these years of suffering as a *corporal*, humiliated, not a single note composed . . .'.

In fact he had taken up serious work again on *Wozzeck* in the summer of 1917, and his degrading experiences as a soldier had a timely influence on his work. A year after that he wrote to his wife: 'There is a bit of me in [Wozzeck's] character, since I have been spending these war years just as dependent on people I hate, have been in chains, sick, captive, resigned, humiliated.' He did not need to add that there is no mention of a war in the twenty-five scenes of Büchner's play, let alone in the fifteen which he adapted for the libretto of his own opera: for Büchner and Berg alike, Wozzeck's daily existence is that of Everyman under arms, at the mercy of a world gone mad.

In the summer of 1918, Berg wrote to his close friend Anton Webern that he was beginning to plan the formal organization of the opera, an organization that would later be seen as one of its most revolutionary aspects. At the time of the Armistice, in November, Schönberg, who had been demobilized the year before, was in Vienna with a fascinating project which became the famous Society for Private Musical Performances. In December, Berg was appointed musical director of this society, and put in charge of concert planning and business affairs. These activities, plus some private teaching, took up most of his time, and work on *Wozzeck* was slowed. (In any case, he did not consult Schönberg about *Wozzeck*, after Schönberg had told him that it was unsuitable for operatic treatment, and that the name 'Wozzeck' was unsingable!)

Berg worked steadily on the opera, and in October 1921 the short score was complete. By the spring of 1922, he had finished the orchestral score, and his pupil, Fritz Heinrich Klein, was working on the piano reduction. Berg had sufficient confidence in his accomplishment to take the considerable financial

11

risk of having the complicated 230-page piano-vocal score engraved at his own expense, borrowing part of the money to cover the cost, and inviting interested people to purchase the score from him by subscription. (In the spring of 1923 both *Wozzeck* and the Three Pieces for Orchestra were taken over by Universal Edition.) Alma Mahler, the widow of Gustav Mahler, gave Berg the money to repay the debt, and in gratitude he dedicated the opera to her.

The new publication soon gained an underground circulation but Berg's reputation was still that of a composer in the orbit of Schönberg, the dangerous radical. Nevertheless, after Webern conducted the first performance, in 1923, of two of Berg's Three Pieces, Opus 6, curiosity about the opera increased. The conductor Hermann Scherchen, who had heard the performance, asked Berg to prepare a set of excerpts from the opera for concert use, and the performance of these 'Three Excerpts from *Wozzeck*' in Frankfurt in 1924 was successful. Meanwhile Erich Kleiber, the newly-appointed director of the Berlin Opera, had listened to the opera played on the piano. According to Willi Reich, after hearing just two scenes Kleiber was so impressed that he exclaimed: 'I am going to do the opera in Berlin even if it costs me my job!'

It almost did cost Kleiber his job, not only because of the novelty of the musical language and its unprecedented technical difficulty, but also because of political machinations within the Berlin Opera management. Thirty-four full orchestral rehearsals were necessary — a nearly unthinkable number then, and absolutely unthinkable now — but on December 14, 1925, the opera was produced at last, the first of seven performances in the season. All were an instant success with the public, just as they were vociferously denounced by most of the critical establishment. Paul Zschorlich's review in the *Deutsche Zeitung* was typical:

> As I was leaving the State Opera, I had the sensation of having been not in a public theatre but in an insane asylum. On the stage, in the orchestra, in the stalls — plain madmen. . . . *Wozzeck* might have been the work of a Viennese Chinaman. For all these mass attacks and instrumental assaults have nothing to do with European music and musical evolution. . . . One may ask oneself seriously to what degree music may be a criminal occupation. We deal here, from a musical viewpoint, with a capital offence.

The success of *Wozzeck* in Berlin was widely reported in the world press. Within a year the opera was produced in Prague under the direction of Otakar Ostrčil, interrupted by a riot which curtailed the number of performances; a third production followed in 1927 in Leningrad. During the next few years the opera was taken up by many other companies throughout Europe, including Berg's own Vienna in 1930 under Clemens Kraus, and in New York and Philadelphia in 1931 directed by Leopold Stokowski. As the first popular success of a substantially atonal work by a composer of the Schönberg circle, *Wozzeck* brought to Berg a worldwide recognition and even a decent income from royalties and performance fees. Berg's standard of living, which had been modest and sometimes precarious ever since his youth, now improved to the extent that he could buy an English Ford car and a summer house in California, the 'Waldhaus' on the Wörthersee; above all, he could afford more time to compose.

During the 1930s Berg was preoccupied with the composition of his second opera, *Lulu*, based on two plays of Frank Wedekind. At the same time, Berg's relatively affluent situation began to deteriorate with the advent of world-wide economic depression and increasing political unrest in Central Europe. When

Set design by Robert Edmund Jones for Act One, scene four (the Doctor's study), for the US première, Philadelphia, 1931 (photo: Archiv Universal Edition)

the Nazis came to power in Germany, Berg's works, like those of most of his contemporaries, were banned there as 'degenerate music', and his royalties began to dwindle. Berg was already in severely strained financial circumstances when he accepted the commission from the American violinist Louis Krasner for his Violin Concerto in the spring of 1935. After completing this, his last work, in only a few months, Berg died of septicaemia on December 23, 1935, at the age of fifty, leaving the final Act of *Lulu* fully composed but not completely written out in orchestral score.

The annexation of Austria to the Third Reich in the spring of 1938 effectively put a stop to performances of any of Berg's major works until after World War II. There were few exceptions, notably the politically courageous production of *Wozzeck* in 1942 in Rome under the direction of Tullio Serafin, with Tito Gobbi in the title role. Within a few years after the end of the war, however, Berg's works were again being widely performed in Europe and America, and the significance of his achievement, not only in relation to Schönberg's and Webern's music but for twentieth-century music generally, was recognised by professionals and public alike. By 1952 *Wozzeck* was available on a commercial recording, superlatively directed by Dmitri Mitropoulos, and five other recordings have appeared since. The opera has been the subject of hundreds of scholarly and popular articles and half a dozen book-length studies, of which the volume by George Perle is outstanding.

As a challenge to the enquiring musical intellect, *Wozzeck* has exerted a fascination among professional musicians ever since the score was published. Berg's own *Lulu*, the only other opera that might be compared with *Wozzeck* from the formal standpoint, has not generated a comparable interest until relatively recently, especially since the availability of the third Act; nor does *Lulu* make the same kind of dramatic impression as its hard-bitten predecessor. It is fair to say that *Wozzeck* has been a monument of operatic history in our century, as much as Wagner's *Tristan and Isolde* was in the nineteenth century, and Büchner's special and visionary dramaturgy bears responsibility for this, hardly less than Berg's uniquely appropriate musical realization. The most obvious influences of *Wozzeck* are to be felt in the German-speaking operatic world, especially in the postwar works of such composers as Henze and von Einem, but also in the operas of Shostakovich, Dallapiccola, and Britten. Even Igor Stravinsky, whose own opera *The Rake's Progress* of 1951 was completely unaffected by the example of *Wozzeck*, acknowledged the central importance of Berg's accomplishment in the evolution of twentieth-century opera, and his own last stage work, *The Flood* of 1962, is indirectly a compliment to Berg.

Yet most composers of today would agree that the liberating force of *Wozzeck* in sound and substance has been felt just as much in non-operatic music as it has been in opera. This rigorous and abstractly conceived operatic structure has nurtured some of the most uninhibited music of all time.

One of the sets of the first production in Prague, 1926, designed by Vlastislav Hofman (photo: National Theatre Archives, Prague)

Georg Büchner's 'Woyzeck': an Interpretation

Kenneth Segar

When Büchner died on February 19, 1837, the manuscript of *Woyzeck* lay uncompleted and in some confusion. It is a moot point whether that confusion has been eliminated from any of the printed versions of the text available today. Most problematic of all is whether the play would have been extended to include the trial and execution of Woyzeck, that is to say, follow the destiny of the historical Johann Christian Woyzeck who was executed on August 27, 1824, for the murder of his mistress, Johanna Christiane Woost. And here it is important to note that in the first published version, that of 1879, Karl Emil Franzos added the stage direction 'drowns', for which there is no manuscript evidence. Even if Woyzeck does not drown, however, there is no need to suppose that the Dissecting Room scene, where a judge and a doctor comment on the murder ('A good murder, a real murder, a beautiful murder . . .') was to form the basis of a potentially anti-climactic continuation of the drama. It could easily be seen as the ultimate expression of society's heartlessness, and a fitting ending to a play that has shown the suffering of a downtrodden misfit at the hands of the privileged class here reacting with brutal indifference to his dead victim. Büchner uses the two executioners finishing a day's work at the guillotine at the end of *Danton's Death* to express indifference to tragic destiny, whose significance the contrast can only heighten.

There is a similar problem about the beginning of the play. The editions of Fritz Bergemann (1949) and Margaret Jacobs (1954) start the play with the scene in which Woyzeck is shaving the Captain, thus laying emphasis on the social context. W.R. Lehmann (1967) and again Margaret Jacobs (1971) choose the scene 'Open country. The town in the distance', in which Woyzeck's hallucinations and apocalyptic visions place in the foreground both his psychological state and his implied questions about the human condition. But, in fact, neither our doubts about the beginning and end of the play nor the disconnectedness of its scenes (of which more later) create any problem of meaning. And this is for the simple reason that the conception of the work is not so much one of linear development as of strands of significance continuously woven together. In whatever order the scenes are placed, no version of the work can avoid creating this texture. Of what do these strands consist? Three are clearly observable: (1) a psychological study raising questions about how we understand personality; (2) a social document containing a satirical critique; (3) a symbolic representation of existential questions — our relationship to the world we inhabit, free will and determinism, idealism and realism.

The psychological study is rooted in the debate surrounding two reports (1821/1823) made on Johann Christian Woyzeck by the psychiatrist Hofrat Dr Clarus at the request of the Leipzig Court. This later interested Büchner, who was a medical student at Giessen, then a lecturer in natural sciences at Zürich University, and whose doctoral dissertation was in the field of comparative anatomy. The issue is whether Woyzeck acted with diminished responsibility, which Clarus declined to accept and so became the instrument of Woyzeck's execution. The polemic in which the psychiatric world thereupon engaged offers a fascinating picture of the state of psychology in the 1820s. But our particular concern here must be with what it was that caused Büchner so to take exception to Clarus' method that he chose to satirise it with comic brutality in his drama *Woyzeck*. For although there is in that satire an

15

Scene from the 1942 Rome production in which Tito Gobbi appeared as Wozzeck (photo: Archiv Universal Edition)

allusion to his own anatomy professor at Giessen, Wilbrand, it is clearly the methodological position of Clarus which the Doctor figure articulates. Quite simply, Büchner objects to any attempt to understand the complexity of a personality *from the outside*, in terms of scientific and moral categories of the day. He satirises the way Clarus lists aspects of anatomy and physiology — build, hair, eyes, pulse, breathing, posture, constitution — by making the Doctor note Woyzeck's reactions to his torment at the hands of the Captain as: 'Watch your pulse-rate, Woyzeck! Fast, heavy beat, irregular.' Or: 'Face muscles taut, rigid. Eye vacant.' Equally anathema is Clarus' listing of mental capacities which are tantamount to a moral sense — self-control, attention, grasp, judgement — and his consequent rejection of Woyzeck, whom he describes as 'morally derelict, all natural feeling blunted, indifferent to the present and the future, lacking religious sense . . . nothing inner or outer to hold him in check.' This disjunction between crude physicality and high-minded morality reflects the poles of scientific materialism and an older philosophical idealism warring for hegemony in contemporary culture. Whilst Büchner insists that we must never overlook our physical reality and should stop talking the cant of Idealism (his character Lenz cries: 'This Idealism is the most shameful contempt for human nature'), it is the way medical science unreflectingly conflates the two perspectives which his best lampoon of the

Doctor turns into grotesque comedy: 'Haven't I proved that the musculus constrictor vesicae is controlled by willpower? Nature indeed! Human beings, Woyzeck, have freedom. Human beings are where individuality is transfigured into freedom. Not control your bladder indeed!'

Büchner counters what he sees as an empty approach by asking us to enter imaginatively into the mind and existence of Woyzeck, for only then shall we have any understanding of his condition. Again to quote the words of his fictional Lenz: 'You have to love human beings so that you can get inside the peculiar personality of each and every one, and none must be thought too insignificant or too ugly; it is the only way to understand them.' Thus Büchner shows us Woyzeck's condition *from the inside*: Woyzeck is tormented by his imperfect relationships, frightened of freemasons and strange mushrooms, seared by sounds and colours of appalling intensity, haunted by visions of death and destruction, plagued by voices. But what Büchner also shows us is that a mentally aberrant person does not cease to be fully human, and indeed that such a person is in one sense more profoundly human, since he or she reveals greater sensitivity, greater capacity to be wounded and ultimately destroyed by an intensely experienced but unanswerable reality. This empathy is a radical challenge to the theory and practice of psychological investigation and understanding in Büchner's time and will have to await the twentieth century to be taken up by phenomenological and existential psychology.

As social document and satirical critique the work looks at Woyzeck as poor, downtrodden, and exploited by his social superiors. There is no doubt that we are meant to recognise the world of privilege in the Captain, the Doctor and the Drum Major, all of whom show their contempt for Woyzeck. The Captain talks down to Woyzeck with his pseudo-morality, philosophical nonsense and mocking allusions to Marie's infidelity; the Doctor is able to misuse Woyzeck for his foolish experiments, and ridicule him into the bargain, because the man needs the pittance to support his mistress and child; the Drum Major has the wealth to tempt Marie with ear-rings, and the status publicly to humiliate Woyzeck. The latter makes the point to the Captain that 'morality' costs money and he is a 'poor devil'. We know that Büchner's sympathies were with the Fourth Estate and that, as a letter to his family reveals, contempt for the lower orders always brought out his hatred for those showing such contempt. He had already produced his revolutionary pamphlet *The Hessian Messenger* (March 1834), and on New Year's Day 1836 he had written to his family about the ragged, freezing children at the Strasbourg Christmas Fair. He concluded: 'The thought that for the majority of people even the humblest pleasures and delights are riches beyond their wildest dreams made me feel very bitter.' At all events, the 'poor little worm', Woyzeck's son, has little that is different to look forward to. The orphaned child at the close (in one manuscript) will have to learn his father's 'Yes, yes, Captain' if he is to achieve even that miserable purchase on material existence. We have, then, in a satirical handling of the élite and the patient suffering of Woyzeck at their hands, writing in the moralist tradition. Yet there is equally a strong Realist depiction. Büchner shows himself to be both a forerunner of the German Naturalist dramatists of the 1880s and 1890s with their insistence on the degrading power of environment and, as the scene where Woyzeck is shaving the Captain metaphorically suggests (the poor man with his knife at the throat of the well-to-do!), an exponent of the idea of society as riven by potential class conflict.

The text is, however, not exhausted by its psychological and social levels. It also tells us what it is to be human in the largest sense, and that means for

17

Büchner that we are vulnerable, suffering creatures, helpless in the face of our own nature and the chaos that is the cosmos. This statement is made through a patterning of language and imagery which permeates the entire text and is drawn from four main sources.

The first of these is the language of increasing materialism in the early nineteenth century. True, as we have seen, the anatomical and physiological terminology of the Doctor, like the Fairground Barker's 'Man, be natural. You were created of dust, sand, muck. Do you want to be more than dust, sand, muck?'[1], are caricature exaggerations in their inability to do justice to the complexity of our humanity, but they nonetheless point to the inescapable bedrock of our physical being. Woyzeck's 'When nature calls', in answer to the Doctor's complaint that he has urinated against a wall and not into his specimen bottle, pays tribute to biological necessity. Büchner may well regret the inadequacy of applying the scientific methods of his day to the human species but, as one schooled in physiology and neurology, he does not hesitate to magnify biological necessity in order to attack the empty phrases of German Idealism. This is underlined in the scene with the Booth-Owner's horse, which is, 'with its tail hanging down and standing on four legs, a member of every learned society . . . this is no brutish individual, this is a person, a human being, a bestial human being — and yet still a beast, a "bête".'

Secondly, there is the language of folksong and fairytale to universalise the characters' experiences into aspects of the human condition. Marie sings of sensuality and childbirth out of wedlock ('Close up shop, my girl, a gypsy boy is coming round' and 'What are you up to, my girl?'); Andres sings of promiscuity ('The landlady's got a good serving wench'); Woyzeck sings of man's lot as one of pain ('Suffering shall be my only gain'), which is not folk-song but a popular hymn of the 1730s; the old man's song at the opening of 'An open place. Booths' ('There's no stay in the world') speaks of transience; and, finally, the grandmother's ghastly fairytale to the 'little mites' shows the small boy crying over the utter desolation of the world and utter isolation of humankind; all hope of an eternal, paradisial order is revealed as delusion; a cruel, crushing emptiness and meaninglessness are what remain.

Thirdly, the language and imagery of the Bible powerfully pose questions about the spiritual life. Marie is found leafing through the Bible and faltering over the story of the woman taken in adultery (John VIII, vv.3-11); with her cry of 'My God, my God, I cannot. My God, only give me the strength to pray', she senses her inability to 'go, and sin no more.' Woyzeck, in the scene 'Street', where the Captain jokes at his expense, speaks of an earth that is 'hot as hell itself' or, in the uncanny scene 'Open fields. The town in the distance', it is an apocalyptic vision — Sodom and Gomorrah, Last Judgement trumpets. This imagery, pointing beyond the personal and social dimensions of the work, embraces humankind's spiritual condition as one of helplessness in the face of things, terror before the strangeness and threatening nature of the cosmos. The pervasive sense is one of damnation rather than redemption. And this metaphysical questioning assumes the authorial voice in the Apprentice's mock sermon 'Why are there human beings?'. Büchner here parodies the prophetic style and, by talking of the human condition in terms of supply/demand/decay, produces a gospel of human misery and anti-faith. The significance of human existence *sub specie aeternitatis* is at stake for Büchner in this comic but fierce interrogation of received truth.

1. All the references to characters and text are to the edition of Büchner's play by Werner R. Lehmann (Hamburg, 1967), and not to the Franzos/Landau edition reprinted here.

Walter Berry as Wozzeck, Vienna, 1955 (photo: Archiv Universal Edition)

Finally, the language of Shakespeare elevates the dark side of the human condition into tragic destiny. Büchner idolised the young Goethe and the J.M.R. Lenz of *The Private Tutor* and *Soldiers*. Both these writers, along with their co-militants of the German Storm and Stress movement of the 1770s, had in their turn idolised Shakespeare. Büchner followed them willingly. Most particularly it is through allusion to *King Lear* and *Othello* that Büchner raises Woyzeck and Marie on to the highest plane of human catastrophe, that of tragic destiny. 'They're doing it in daylight, doing it on your hands like gnats', weeps the betrayed Woyzeck at the sight of Marie and the Drum Major dancing in erotic excitement, an utterance ironically recalling the merciful response of Lear's own broken heart: 'Thou shalt not die! die for adultery! No: / The wren goes to't, and the small gilded fly / Does lecher in my sight. / Let copulation thrive.' But, of course, it is *Othello* which fully articulates the fate of our two protagonists as tragedy. 'The woman is hot, hot', says Woyzeck ('Inn'), recalling Othello's 'hot, hot and moist'. Or in the scene 'By the pool', Woyzeck's 'What hot lips you have, hot like your whore's breath. And yet I'd give up heaven to kiss them one more time' echoes Othello as he kisses Desdemona: 'O balmy breath that does almost persuade / Justice to break her sword! . . . One more and this the last / So sweet was ne'er so fatal.' A final example of Woyzeck-Othello: 'Can't you die? So! So! Ha, she's still breathing; still not dead? still not?' and Othello's 'Not dead? not yet quite dead? / I that am cruel am yet merciful;/ I would not have thee linger in thy pain:— / So, so.' And, of course, in Marie's bible-reading and prayer there is an obvious parallel to Desdemona's willow song. What is remarkable about all this is that Büchner has found a way (without doubt a tribute to Goethe's Gretchen) to make unschooled, barely articulate people give form to attitudes beyond their mental and linguistic grasp. It is no detraction from the psychological and social realism of the work when these characters use biblical utterance, hymns, folksongs and fairytales to articulate life's problems: in life people do just that. Here, the method conjoins with Büchner's allusion to Shakespearean tragic diction to create a web of language and image that, whilst skilfully adapted to the characters' own mode of speech and so avoiding any stylistic break, lyrically elevates these humble protagonists and through them asks the largest questions about our human condition.

So: we have a text in which psychological, social and existential matters are addressed. But these matters do not, of course, appear on discrete levels: the individual is at the same time social being and all humankind; the particular is subsumed into increasingly more general concerns. The genius of the work lies in the way these different facets are presented as interwoven strands, all continuously present throughout. The technique for organising the material is the same disjointed progression found in certain dramas of the German Storm and Stress movement, which leap without transition from one essentially self-contained scene to the next. With those writers, the main preoccupation, apart from breaking with neoclassical form, had been to employ these abrupt shifts as a formal counterpart to the energy and vitality of the protagonists. In *Woyzeck*, however, they are used to create lyrically concentrated substance. (Readers of *Woyzeck* are almost always surprised how little text there is to produce such richness of substance. This concentration of all the dimensions of the work is not progressively created by the drama but is present in microcosm in the multi-valency of almost every scene. To take just two examples: The Grandmother's fairytale mirrors Woyzeck's *psychological* desolation, his child's *social* deprivation, and the *existential* judgement that humankind appears as lost children, without father and mother, without hope. Or take the briefest possible scene 'Barrack Square' (from one of the drafts[2]), where Woyzeck (here called Louis) anticipates the murder of his mistress, already speaking of her in the past tense: '. . . But, Andres, for all that she was still a marvellous girl.' The protagonist's *psychological* state is there in his being torn between vengeance and deepest love; his *social* predicament is there in that he has been robbed of his woman by the richer and more privileged Drum Major; the *existential* condition is there because life is unfair — how could Marie resist sexual attraction to a man like a 'tree', a 'lion'? —and cruel — misery occurs because, as Büchner's Danton says, our suffering results from

2. The Franzos/Landau text conflates this scene, see footnote on page 96.

20

Walter Berry as Wozzeck, Vienna, 1955 (photo: Archiv Universal Edition)

the fact that 'a mistake was made when we were created', pain is existential. Such is Büchner's craft that he can reveal to us in the minutest components of his work that tragedy is not set apart from individual character and social reality.

* * *

That the work is moving is beyond question. But readers frequently ask whether Büchner is a nihilist, who simply states that life is chaos and suffering, and that there is no positive value or indeed meaning in existence. The answer is a resounding 'no'. Büchner, true to his scientific training, is objective in the sense that he does not fudge unpalatable reality but sees issues through to the bitter end, to their ultimate painfulness. Yet this degree of realism and intellectual honesty is itself a value. And I should like to add two more palpable values. Firstly, there is Woyzeck's love, which is given such intensity in the text. This is why, whatever scholarship decrees, the 'Barrack Square' scene with Andres should not be omitted from any reading or acting text — the utterance 'But, Andres, for all that she was still a marvellous girl' tells us that Woyzeck, like Othello, is being driven to kill what he most loves, that this is tragedy, and that tragedy is both terrible and positive, for in the destruction of what we most value we are aware of it as at no other moment. Secondly, there is value in Büchner's compassion. His creed was to be humane. In his literary realism, as we have seen, he spurns the philosophical Idealism of his age to show life as harsh, cruel, unjust. The tenor of Büchner's attitudes, whether social, political or metaphysical, often appears negative or nihilistic but rarely expresses anything other than his moral indignation or bitterness that things should be so. Büchner is precisely of his historical moment, caught between the loss of a spiritual metaphysic and the incapacity of materialism and its burgeoning sciences to explain suffering. Again to quote his figure Lenz, who resents the destruction and pain in the world: 'If I were all-powerful, if I were that, you know, I couldn't bear there to be suffering, I'd save people, I'd save them!' And of all the people whom Büchner's art 'saves' through his compassion, his 'pitying gaze', it is unquestionably the poor, the downtrodden, the outcasts of society who are at the heart of his concern.

Nowhere is this clearer than in his choice, in the 1830s, of a man from the lowest order of society, desperately poor, without hope of betterment, barely articulate, mentally disturbed, as tragic hero. Compared to the other radical transformations which Büchner achieved in the three years before he died at the age of twenty-three — wresting the sixteenth-century religious broadsheet to pre-Marxist needs (*The Hessian Messenger*); rethinking the genre of historical tragedy to make the historical process itself the protagonist (*Danton's Death*); enlarging the scope of psychological narrative to embrace, with brutal realism and passionate empathy, the collapse of a personality into insanity (*Lenz*); mingling Gozzi, Shakespearean and Romantic comedy to create a precursor of absurdist drama (*Leonce and Lena*) — compared to all these radical transformations of traditional literary modes, it is with *Woyzeck* that he surely went furthest in visionary power. The insignificant historical subject of a *fait divers*, the impoverished, brutish, drunken, violent Johann Christian Woyzeck, who savagely killed his mistress in a doorway, became transfigured in a work that is — an unheard-of hybrid genre — at once humanitarian satire and proletarian lyric tragedy. Contemplating the supreme originality of this creative act, of discovering so much human resonance in the 'lowest of the low', Elias Canetti, in accepting the Büchner Prize in 1972, said: 'with *Woyzeck* Büchner achieved the most complete revolution in the whole of literature.'

Hermann Uhde (Wozzeck) and Paul Franke (Captain) in the Metropolitan Opera première by Herbert Graf, designed by Caspar Neher, conducted by Karl Böhm, 1959 (photo: Louis Mélançon)

22

'Wozzeck': The Musico-Dramatic Structure

This chart of the musico-dramatic structure of the opera was prepared by
Fritz Mahler, a pupil of Berg, who approved of it and made sure it was
included in all copies of the 1923 vocal score sent to critics.

Drama		Music
	ACT ONE	
Expositions		**Five character pieces**
Wozzeck in relation to his environment		
Wozzeck and the Captain	**Scene One**	Suite
Wozzeck and Andres	**Scene Two**	Rhapsody
Wozzeck and Marie	**Scene Three**	Military March and Lullaby
Wozzeck and the Doctor	**Scene Four**	Passacaglia
Marie and the Drum Major	**Scene Five**	Andante affettuoso (quasi Rondo)
	ACT TWO	
Dramatic development		**Symphony in five movements**
Marie and her child, later Wozzeck	**Scene One**	Sonata movement
The Captain and the Doctor, later Wozzeck	**Scene Two**	Fantasia and fugue
Marie and Wozzeck	**Scene Three**	Largo
Garden of an inn	**Scene Four**	Scherzo
Guard room in the barracks	**Scene Five**	Rondo con introduzione
	ACT THREE	
Catastrophe and epilogue		**Six inventions**
Marie and her child	**Scene One**	Invention on a theme
Marie and Wozzeck	**Scene Two**	Invention on a note
A low bar	**Scene Three**	Invention on a rhythm
Death of Wozzeck	**Scene Four**	Invention on a hexachord
	Orchestral interlude: Invention on a key	
Children playing	**Scene Five**	Invention on a regular quaver movement

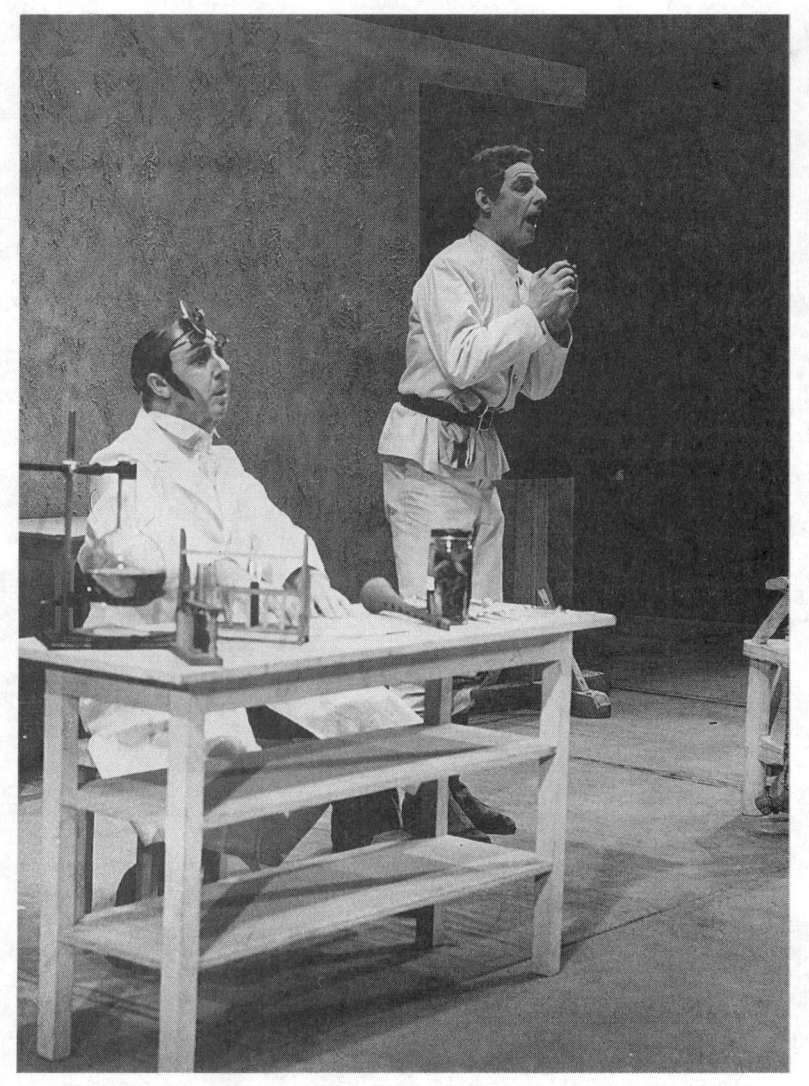

Karl Dönch (Doctor) and Hermann Uhde (Wozzeck), Metropolitan Opera, 1959 (photo: Louis Mélançon)

Musical Form and Dramatic Expression in Alban Berg's 'Wozzeck'

Theo Hirsbrunner

Alban Berg first saw Georg Büchner's *Woyzeck* (then entitled *Wozzeck*) on May 5, 1914, and was deeply impressed. That text, based on the edition by Karl Emil Franzos, included only some of the fragments that Büchner had left unfinished at the time of his death. Berg actually saw only the fragment of a fragment, in which the original order of the scenes could not be established with any certainty. From the outset, there was a problem of what formal structure the opera should have.

This was not a new problem for a composer. Wagner had not constructed his mature music dramas from arias and ensembles divided by recitatives. From *The Ring* onwards, he ensured musical coherency through a dense system of leitmotifs, although he did not altogether abandon periodic structure with its regular divisions of vocal lines in four or eight bar groups (Siegmund's Spring Song, for example). He wrote his alliterative texts in poetically heightened prose rather than in metrically regular lines with end-rhyme; and because they were conceived to be set to music, there could be a fundamental interaction between the dramatic poem and the score. Indeed, the result owed more to Beethoven's symphonic style than to earlier operatic music. What was important to Wagner in the formal structure was the development of short musical ideas rather than the juxtaposition of easily retainable melodies. His contemporaries complained about the lack of form in his music dramas because they failed to recognise what was there as itself a new form.

Wagner's achievements posed a significant problem for subsequent opera composers: neither Claude Debussy, for instance, nor Richard Strauss wrote his own texts. Both instead set plays that had been written in prose for the spoken theatre: Debussy chose Maurice Maeterlinck's *Pelléas and Mélisande*, Strauss chose Oscar Wilde's *Salome*. Yet neither playwright abandoned the lofty style which they considered indispensable to tragedy. In this, as much as in the choice of subject matter, they differed from Büchner, who had used everyday speech patterns in *Wozzeck* and allowed his characters to speak the language of the underprivileged. This prompted Berg's teacher, Arnold Schönberg, to comment, when he heard of Berg's plan to base an opera on the play, that music should concern itself with angels rather than orderlies. Music, at least the kind of music being written by Schönberg and Berg in the wake of late Romanticism, seemed ill-suited to setting a text with realistic dialogue. Rhetoric is totally absent from *Wozzeck*, where the dominant mood is one of speechlessness, and where the characters are unable to articulate at all adequately. They never step back and reflect on the situations in which they are embroiled. They know only ignorance, cynicism and sensual appetite, expressing themselves in protests of indignation and quotations from the Bible.

Berg nonetheless succeeded in dividing the play into three groups of five scenes each and in giving them a relatively clear-cut musical form. Sonata form, fugue, rondo, suite, passacaglia and so on give a bone-structure to Büchner's fragmentary play. Working very slowly, Berg rearranged the text, combining scenes and abridging the dialogue, but adding very little of his own. Perhaps he resembles Wozzeck himself in this, for Wozzeck believes he can see 'circular lines' and 'figures' between the mushrooms growing in the forest. But for 'poor Wozzeck' these fantasies are attempts to bring some sense of order to an already troubled mind, whereas for Berg they evolved into a system of associations of unprecedented complexity. He made up what amounts to a secret musical code. Anyone studying the score in detail will discover a network of esoteric allusions of a kind that recurs in the Lyric Suite for string quartet and in his second opera *Lulu*. But even an audience not initiated into these arcane mysteries will appreciate the music's dramatic appeal, immediately convincing and moving. It never seems to be cerebral. By a process of osmosis the music merges with the action, and the brief scenes of the drama stand out from one another, while forming a dense and unified whole.

Although Berg began the opera immediately after seeing the play in 1914, he did not complete the score until the early 1920s. Just before he took his initial

Geraint Evans as Wozzeck, Covent Garden, 1960 (photo: Houston Rogers/Royal Opera House Archives)

steps he experienced a compositional crisis provoked by Schönberg's violent criticism of his pupil's tendency towards aphoristic utterances (most notably in the Altenberg Lieder and the Four Pieces for clarinet and piano). Schönberg believed that each of his students ought to write at least one symphony, and Berg did, in fact, start to do so but got no further than a handful of sketches which are strongly influenced by Mahler. *Wozzeck*, however, allowed Berg to incorporate marches and folksongs into a large-scale form; if only in this inclination to mix high and low styles, he may be seen as Mahler's successor. With both composers, however, their 'popular' music is never merely superficial because they introduced dissonances which raise it to the level of 'serious' music. Even in the nineteenth century, opera drew on different stylistic registers to express dramatic action. By contrast with the Classical sonata form or the Baroque fugue, such music was 'impure', and yet it is precisely these forms of 'pure' music which Berg incorporated in *Wozzeck*. These structures are not immediately audible but emerge only from a reading of the score. Yet their characteristics are astonishingly appropriate to the drama. Even in instrumental works musical forms are not just shells to be filled with random content; they have the characteristics of identifiable psychological states. For example, the fugue and passacaglia forms are cerebral and erudite, the scherzo is dance-like, and the slow movement of a symphony or sonata lends itself to the deepest and most intense emotions. Aware of this, Berg wrote a score in which the formal structures are themselves *musically* expressive.

*

When the curtain rises on Act One Wozzeck is shaving the Captain. The Captain talks to himself, indulges in a spot of amateur philosophising, comments on the weather and lectures Wozzeck on the latter's illegitimate child. Wozzeck justifies himself by reminding the Captain that he has insufficient money to marry. This scene is written in the form of a Suite, which since the seventeenth century has been a sequence of the most disparate dance movements or vocal numbers. The opening is a Prelude and the final section a Postlude, which is an exact retrograde of the Prelude, that is to say it is the same note for note but played backwards. Within this framework the dances — a Sarabande, a Gigue and a Gavotte — unfold, culminating in an Air. The sections are linked by bridge passages, just as the whole scene is held together by Wozzeck's taciturn answer, 'Jawohl, Herr Hauptmann' ('Yes, Sir. Quite so, Sir!'), which is always articulated on the same note and in the same rhythm:

WOZZECK

Sehr mäßige Vierte.

Ja – wohl. Herr Haupt – mann!
Yes, Sir. Quite so, Sir!

The form as a whole is thus recognisable. The rhythm and the note are endlessly repeated, in greatly intensified form, throughout the music that follows, until the curtain goes up on the next scene. We are now outside the town, at the edge of the wood, where Wozzeck and his friend Andres are cutting sticks for the Captain. A Rhapsody on three chords is interrupted from time to time by Andres' hunting song. There is a marked contrast between

Wozzeck's fearful imaginings and Andres' carefree attitude. Wozzeck speaks of the threat of the freemasons and of the glow of the setting sun, while his companion sings to dispel his anxieties. Because of Berg's tendency to mediate between opposites, their emotional states are not wholly unrelated. At the beginning of the song about the huntsman's carefree life we hear two of the chords from the Rhapsody which echo Wozzeck's sombre mood. Andres sings pitifully off-key, failing to find the folk-song's simple melody and setting up resonances with Mahler's symphonies and with *Des Knaben Wunderhorn*:

The transition to the following scene is a masterpiece of what Wagner called the 'art of transition': the three chords of the Rhapsody are overlaid by trumpet signals from the barracks in the town, and already we see the Drum Major marching past with his bandsmen. Marie nods a friendly greeting to him, joining in the march and singing the words, 'Soldaten, Soldaten sind schöne Burschen!' ('The soldiers, the soldiers are handsome fellows!'). These words are an inexact quotation from Mahler's song 'Revelge', where the same melody is first sung to the words, 'Ach, Bruder, ach Bruder, ich kann dich nicht tragen' ('My brother, my brother, I cannot bear you away'). In the Mahler, too, we are dealing with the cliché of popular music transformed into something more 'serious' by changes in its form. The second section of this scene takes place inside Marie's room, where she has withdrawn to escape her neighbour's abuse. Wozzeck enters; the chords which announce him will later accompany Marie's death in Act Three, scene two:

It is Wozzeck himself who will kill her. Even here, during their first meeting in the opera, he inspires fear. Not even the lullaby that Marie sings shortly beforehand to the child (whom she describes as having an 'unehrliches

Gesicht', lit. dishonest face) can conceal her panic, and she rushes from the room.

The next scene takes place at the Doctor's. The Doctor hopes to enhance his scientific reputation by carrying out medical experiments on Wozzeck. This music is therefore written in the strict form of a Passacaglia with twenty-one Variations. An elaborate network of associations between different musical ideas is developed over a bass line made up of the twelve notes of the chromatic scale, and this passacaglia outdoes anything that earlier composers such as Purcell and Bach had done with the form. And yet the music follows Büchner's text very closely. For example, Wozzeck attempts to describe his visions in order to make them credible to the Doctor, even though he cannot really believe in them himself. As he sings the words, 'wenn was is und doch nicht is' ('when it's there and is not there!'), the twelve notes of the theme are rapidly recapitulated; it can no longer strictly be described as the original theme, since what the notes now form is a variation upon it. On the other hand, they scarcely make a full variation since it is the merest hint, just a phantom. Text and music mirror one another perfectly.

When Wozzeck tells the Doctor about the mysterious mushrooms in the forest and when he tries to read a message into the 'circular lines' and 'figures' that they form, the orchestra indulges in symmetrical circular movements, while the following theme is heard on the first trumpet:

Berg has compressed this twelfth variation into a single bar in order to emphasise its central importance for the work. In a sense this is music for the eye rather than the ear, yet it is not without a sensual appeal that communicates itself directly to the listener.

The fifth and final scene of this opening Act is an *Andante affetuoso* in rondo form, its constant repetitions implying the Drum Major's insistent approaches to Marie. The music is much simpler, much more direct; lyrical sections alternate with trumpet fanfares expressing his military arrogance. He appeals to the instinctive, weak-willed Marie and, at the moment of his conquest, the orchestra unfurls its whole tremendous force, a force which indicates not redemption through love and transfiguring death, but cruel annihilation in a world without pity. That Marie no less than Wozzeck will come to such an end is anticipated in the music that ends the first Act.

The second Act is written in the form of a five-movement symphony: Sonata, Fugue, Adagio, Scherzo and Rondo succeed each other without a break as in Schönberg's Chamber Symphony, Opus 9. This way the links between the movements become even closer than in Beethoven's Classical symphonic model.

The first scene corresponds more or less exactly to the popular conception of sonata form. The opening theme consists of brief motifs, while the second is more overtly tuneful as Marie sings a simple song to her infant son. Her confrontation with Wozzeck coincides with the development section, which is characteristically full of musical conflicts. It culminates unexpectedly in a C-major chord when Wozzeck mentions the money that he has earned from the Captain and Doctor. Through the works of other composers this chord is associated with the shining luminosity of gold — in Haydn's *Creation*, for example, on the word 'light', when the chorus sings, 'and there was light', or in Wagner's *Rhinegold* when the sun's rays catch the gold on the bed of the Rhine and cause it to glow. For Berg, this chord has lost its divine and magical significance, and symbolises only filthy lucre. It will reappear in *Lulu* when Dr Schön announces that he has to go to the stock-exchange.

The second scene is a Triple Fugue — triple because it involves three characters, the Captain, the Doctor and Wozzeck, meeting in the street. At the beginning of the scene the two themes that had been associated with the Captain and the Doctor are heard simultaneously in the orchestra. The Captain's theme, pretentious in character, is in the upper part, while the Doctor's theme, calm and dignified, proceeds in the lower line:

Later Wozzeck's gloomy and sluggish theme is added:

Highly complex structures develop as Wozzeck deduces from their cynical remarks that Marie has been unfaithful. The dense confusion of the orchestral writing has something disturbing about it which, far from being an end in itself, mirrors the tension that runs through the dialogue.

The third scene shows Wozzeck returning to Marie's house. Provocatively, insisting on her right to love whomever she likes, she rouses Wozzeck's jealousy, causing him to threaten her, even though he is still besotted with her. It is mainly accompanied by a chamber orchestra using the same distribution as Schönberg's Chamber Symphony, Opus 9. When Wozzeck, in his despair,

30

sings the words, 'Der Mensch ist ein Abgrund' ('Man is a chasm'), the instrumental lines plunge to their lowest register, evoking the sense of being cursed and lost that weighs so heavily on all the characters:

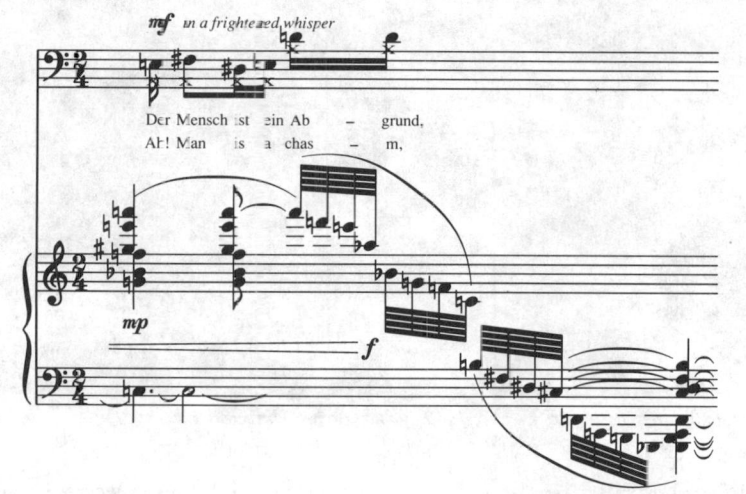

WOZZECK

Noch langsamer

Der Mensch ist ein Ab — grund,
Ah! Man is a chas — m,

The fourth scene takes place in a beer-garden where people are dancing, drinking and speechifying wildly. Wozzeck sees Marie dancing with the Drum Major, who holds her tightly in his arms. He stops himself from rushing headlong after them, waiting to kill her later. Waltzes, Ländler and folksongs alternate with recitative-like sections. The on-stage band contains between two and four fiddles (violins strung with steel strings and tuned a whole tone higher than normal), an accordion and a bombardon. Mahler had also used the thin, attenuated sound of fiddles in his symphonies but there are allusions to other composers in this Scherzo. One of the waltz melodies recalls the one in Strauss's *Der Rosenkavalier* when Ochs tries to woo Sophie, 'Mit mir, mit mir keine Kammer dir zu klein . . .' ('With me, with me no chamber too small for you . . .'), and later we hear the first bar of the Minuet from the Act One finale of Mozart's *Don Giovanni*. These two references to operatic seductions are transplanted from the aristocratic world to a vulgar beer-garden in much the same way that the C-major chord in Act Two, scene one, has lost the sublime quality that it had for Haydn and Wagner.

Frenzied dance music leads into the next scene, which takes place in the soldiers' dormitory. Wozzeck is unable to sleep and is beaten and humiliated by the drunken Drum Major, who boasts of his latest conquest. In their sleep the other soldiers can be heard humming the three chords from the Rhapsody in Act One, scene two. As the Act ends, the Drum Major's brutal music gives way to total silence, a silence which seems to say more about Wozzeck's hopelessness than any notes ever could.

The orchestra is also silent as the curtain rises on the third and final Act which, from a formal point of view, is the most original of the three. Berg simply calls the scenes 'Inventions' — inventions on a theme, a single note, a rhythm, a chord, a key (as an interlude before the final scene) and on a continuous quaver movement. In the first scene we find Marie reading a passage from the Bible about the woman taken in adultery whom Christ

Christa Ludwig as Marie, Vienna, 1963 (photo: Archiv Universal Edition)

forgives her sins. She also tells her child a story to lull him to sleep. These passages are of the greatest simplicity and written in the tonal style which Berg had already superseded. This gives them a certain archaic character, whereas Marie's outbursts of despair and her guilty conscience are portrayed in atonal music.

The second scene is the freest in terms of form: only the note of B natural, repeated at different octaves, stabilises the music, which reacts with seismographic accuracy to every fluctuation in the text — to the night dew as it falls on the grass, to Marie's sense of unease and to the moon which seems to Wozzeck like a piece of blood-stained iron. As he stabs Marie, the orchestra once again repeats all her musical themes, followed by the chords which had been heard in Act One, scene three, when she was waiting for him. In a postlude to the scene the single note of B natural is subjected to a *crescendo* of unbearable intensity until finally all we hear is this single note.

It is impossible to think of a more glaring contrast between this and the following scene, in the inn. There is, none the less, an esoteric link with the B natural that has just died away in that the entries of the various instruments had echoed the rhythm of a polka which is now taken up on an out-of-tune pianino:

SCHNELLPOLKA
(on out-of-tune Piano on stage)

This rhythm remains audible in the orchestra and in the vocal line throughout the scene, sometimes slow, sometimes fast. Berg invented this kind of structure. While Schönberg always set out from particular pitches, investing them with a sense of rhythm only as the work developed, Berg adopted the opposite course in certain sections of *Lulu* and in the whole of his Violin Concerto: he placed rhythm before all else and only later devised the melodies and chords to go with it. In this way he became one of the precursors of serialism in which pitch and rhythm are granted equal status. But no one would guess that the same polka rhythm could be adapted in the course of the scene to suit Wozzeck's insane ramblings, Margret's simple folk-song and the shouts and screams of the crowd. A certain artificiality seems to lend the vocal lines the quality of caricature, a distortion well suited to Wozzeck's despair.

No less exceptional is the fourth scene, consisting entirely of a six-part chord which, initially, is not even transposed. In other words, Berg imposed narrow constraints on himself within which he develops a great variety. The chord is capable, for example, of expressing the croaking of the toads in the pond:

At another point it accompanies the appearance of the moon:

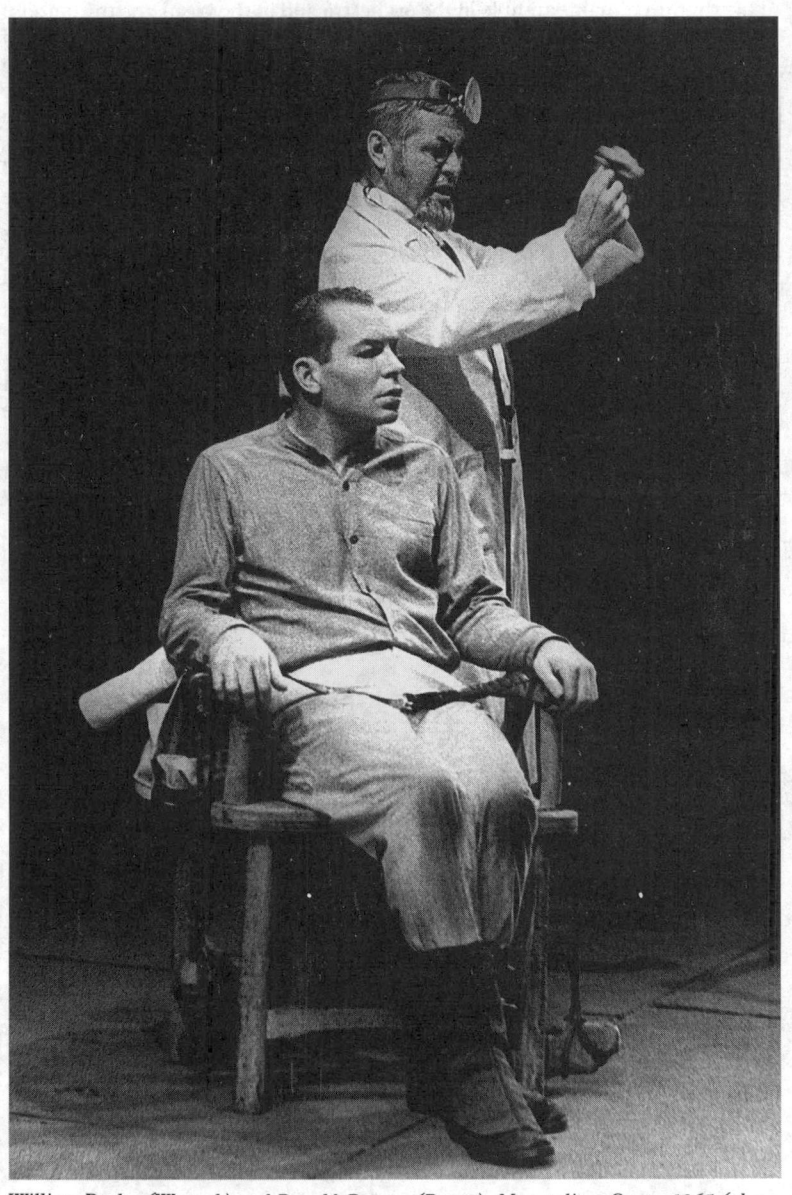

William Dooley (Wozzeck) and Donald Gramm (Doctor), Metropolitan Opera, 1965 (photo: Metropolitan Opera House Archives)

And when the mist rises over the pond in which Wozzeck has drowned, the same chord gradually glides upwards in long ascending lines. The passage is reminiscent of Debussy but it differs from Impressionistic writing in that the structure is prescribed down to the last detail. It is clear from many of his still unpublished works that Berg, as a young man, was deeply influenced by Debussy. Under Schönberg's influence, however, he opted for a rigorous thematic approach to composition, although he never abandoned the tonal sensuality that had attracted him to the French composer.

Berg's preface to the final scene brings together most of the opera's themes in an Invention on the key of D minor. The music sounds like a farewell, a threnody for Wozzeck. For once, compassion and consternation at the terrible fate suffered by these 'poor people' seems to break through. Free of any trace of sentimentality, however, Berg closes with a scene in which the children continue to play games, treating Marie's murder just as an exciting incident. Finally her son remains alone on stage with his hobby-horse; he understands nothing of what has happened, and he is perhaps doomed to as wretched an existence as his parents.

The quaver configuration in the orchestra admits of no *accelerando*, no *crescendo* in these closing moments of the work, but this reticence is far more powerful than any dramatic outcry could have been. After the Invention on the key of D minor, there is nothing left for the final scene to convey except that sense of emptiness and numbness with which the opera ends:

Schluß der Oper

Berg's music is atonal. In the main it is unrelated to any specific key, unlike contemporary works by Debussy, Strauss and Mahler. To give his audience something to hold on to, he had recourse in *Wozzeck* to all these formal musical structures. He even went as far as to end the first Act with the same chord as the final Act. The second Act begins more or less as the first one ends, whereas there is silence between the second and third Acts, during which the curtain remains up. Many other allusions and correspondences in the score could be pointed out. Is *Wozzeck* therefore a work that exists only to be read? The success of the piece in the theatre proves that even music structured along strictly formal lines can be understood by audiences. Berg himself once said in a lecture than if he identified his forms on that occasion, it was so that the audience could ignore them when they listened to the music. Yet it is impossible to ignore them altogether, since their dramatic expressivity is so direct in its appeal.

Christel Goltz (Marie) and Thorsteinn Hannesson (Drum Major) in the first production at Covent Garden, by Sumner Austin with designs by Caspar Neher, conducted by Erich Kleiber, 1952 (photo: Angus McBean © Harvard Theatre Collection)

On the Characteristics of 'Wozzeck'

Theodor W. Adorno

Because both the play and the opera of *Wozzeck* have comparable claims to be considered as important works, the relationship between them is worth considering. Music might be thought to be superfluous to such a poetic text, and merely to replicate its hidden content and the very quality that makes it a poem. The fact that they were written a century apart helps one to understand what Berg's infinitely complex opera has in common with Büchner's intentionally sketchlike fragment and what they share in terms of aesthetic economy. Berg in effect composed what had germinated in the text during all those decades of neglect. That germ gives the music its secret polemic. It seems to be saying that what you, as listeners, have forgotten, indeed what you have never learned, is as strange, as true and as human as I am myself, and that by introducing it to you I am also commending it to you. As an opera *Wozzeck* aims to revise history: it is a process in which history, too, is included; the modernity of the music underlines the modernity of the book precisely because the latter is old and was not recognised in its own day. Just as Büchner did justice to the tortured, confused soldier Woyzeck, who in his dehumanised humanity is exemplary beyond all the accidentals of his person, so in the same way the composer intends to do justice to the play. The passionate care lavished on the minutest detail of its texture reveals the extent to which what one thought was diffuse is formally coherent, how what seemed unfinished is actually a finished piece. This is the function of the music — not to produce psychological effect, to create a mood or impression, although it does not hesitate to do so in order to reveal what lies buried beneath the surface of the work. Hofmannsthal once said of the text of *Der Rosenkavalier* that his 'comedy for music' was precisely that since music was appropriate for showing not what is *in* people but *between* them.

This is even truer of *Wozzeck* in that Berg seems to offer an interlinear version of the text. The opera does not merely interpret the characters' feelings but attempts to communicate what a hundred years have done to Büchner's scenes: it transforms a realist sketch into a text that teems with hidden significance; what the words do not express ensures an increase in content. The music exists to reveal this increase, to reveal what has been omitted. It glides over the fragment with an infinitely gentle touch, soothing and smoothing whatever obtrudes, seeking to comfort the play out of its despair. Everything fits together perfectly. The art of transition is handled with far greater skill than anything Wagner ever imagined by the term, even to the point where everything in the world seems to connect. It is not afraid of extremes: the dark sadness of its South-German-cum-Austrian tone assimilates Büchner's tragedy entirely, but also invests it with a self-contained and immanent form which allows expression and suffering to take on visible shape. In doing so it becomes, as it were, a transcendental court of appeal. The dovetailing and interlocking of the music, its seamlessness, is decisive. If this breaks down in performance, if the fabric is torn even for a second, the sound picture collapses into chaos. What emerges is of course an aspect of the work itself, that stunned *espressivo* which needs the most extreme discipline of construction and sound if it is not to become diffuse. Berg's score exists entirely in a state of tension between the surging unconscious and an almost optically architectonic feeling for enclosed surfaces. He himself described *Wozzeck* as a '*piano* opera' that erupts from time to time in wild emotion. Only now that the printed score is generally accessible is it possible to judge how true this is.

Whole stretches, including the Suite with which the first Act opens, are genuinely chamber-like, scored for solo instruments; only occasionally is a passage set in a highly complex manner, the *tutti* sections being reserved entirely for the few dramatic turning-points in the work. Such economy of sound supports the density of the texture to the utmost through the perfect clarity and unambiguity of every musical event. Without being unduly paradoxical, the work may be said to be simple, even though it has remained difficult and requires so many rehearsals: and this is because not a single note, not a single instrumental voice, is included that is not indispensable to realise its musical meaning, that is, how it all connects. The truly functional style of the writing gives the lie to all those commentators who prate about post-Tristanesque late Romanticism, thus relegating the music to the past because they have not been able to keep abreast of it.

The first thing to be learned from *Wozzeck* is the meaning of the term *ausinstrumentieren* (to work out the score to its finest detail). Even today the ideas that continue to dominate any discussion about orchestration would make a painter, for example, for whom colour is so self-evidently an integral part of his work, shake his head in disbelief. That ghastly concept of a composer's 'brilliant treatment of the orchestra' has, on the one hand, come back into fashion; as though this musical practice (borrowed from horse-trading in that it is designed to dress up the music as colourfully and gaudily as possible in order to conceal its utter feebleness) had not been refuted by the leading exponents of New Music once and for all. On the other hand, those who do not care for false riches cultivate an asceticism which they hope will banish the joy of colour from music and thus reverse the advance of the tonal dimension as an essential compositional element. The *Wozzeck* score acts as a corrective to both these tendencies. The orchestra 'realises' the music in the sense that Cézanne uses the verb 'réaliser'. The entire compositional structure, from its overall organisation to the finest tracery of the motivic writing, is revealed in colour values. Conversely, no colour is used unless it has a precise function in depicting the musical context. The formal structure corresponds at every point to the orchestral disposition: *concertino*-like ensemble combinations and *tutti* effects are carefully balanced. It is a prime example of the art of tonal transition, imperceptibly gliding from one colour to another. But the atmosphere evoked by this orchestration, as it immerses itself, self-forgetful, in the hollow spaces behind Büchner's words, is not mere conjuration of mood. It derives from Berg's capacity for nuance, which is at one with his art of scoring, so that even the tiniest compositional impulse finds a sensory equivalent.

The simplicity of the score is best illustrated, perhaps, by reference to Strauss. In *Ein Heldenleben* and *Salome*, far more happens on the written page than can actually be heard in the orchestra; much of what is written remains ornamental, mere padding. In the case of Berg — because the role of the orchestra is totally subordinate to the musical construction — everything seems almost geometrically clear, as though in some architectural drawing, and the richness of the score is only fully revealed in performance. The score is never superfluous nor fussy, and it provides subtly differentiated sounds which turn out to be the surprisingly obvious solution — such as the impressions of the water in Wozzeck's death scene. What has not been written attests to as great a creative power as what has been written, and it is this economy alone which gives Berg's exuberant musical substance the persuasive power of form. Many scenes which appear particularly complicated in the vocal score, such as the Fantasia and Triple Fugue in the second scene of Act Two, assume a plasticity and transparency in the full score that have not usually been realised in theatrical performance; they were in fact first realised by Boulez.

The closed nature of the structure, which achieves dramatic expressiveness while avoiding crass and primitive contrasts, is obtained through its musical method. *Wozzeck* is the first stage work of any length in which the language of free atonality was spoken. Having abandoned tonality, Berg was obliged to develop other means to produce clear relationships in his music. The means were a motivic and thematic style, derived from the tradition of Viennese Classicism, and transferred to the stage more substantially than ever before. This is the function of a compositional style which is Mahlerian in its clarity. We should underestimate this construction if we were to confuse it with the much-discussed forms of absolute music in *Wozzeck*. Although these are used to organise the score over a relatively broad time-span, they neither need nor ought to be perceived as absolute forms: rather they are invisible, like the rows of a good serial composition in later music. Moreover, the formal links are underlined by a series of graphic leitmotifs altogether typical of Wagnerian music drama; the triple fugue in the street scene in the second Act, for example, combines three of the most important of these motifs, those of the Captain and Doctor, and the faltering triplets of Wozzeck's helplessness. Far more important, however, is the inner composition of the music, its fabric or texture. At the time when *Wozzeck* was written, numerous composers, especially Stravinsky and Hindemith, were striving for a new autonomy in operatic music. They wanted to free it from dependence on the poetic word. In *Wozzeck*, too, the music announces a new claim to autonomy. But Berg's method is the exact opposite of that of the neoclassicists, since it involves an unquestioning absorption in the text. The music of *Wozzeck* is like an extremely rich, diversely structured curve on a graph representing the opera's overall internal development: it is Expressionistic insofar as every musical event refers to an internalised, psychological world. In reproducing every dramatic emotion, the music reaches the point of utter self-effacement. And yet it is developed in as structured, articulate and varied a way as only great music can be, such as the instrumental movements of Brahms or Schönberg. Its autonomy is achieved by unfolding a constant stream of self-sustaining music, whereas those operatic composers who distance themselves from the stage and press relentlessly on in that direction, will find that their works threaten to become for that very reason monotonous and boring. Perhaps it is the deepest paradox of the *Wozzeck* score that it attains to musical autonomy not by offering opposition to the word but by rescuing it and following it with the utmost fidelity. Wagner's demand that the orchestra should reflect every last detail of the drama, and thus become symphonic, is one which *Wozzeck* realises; and this is what finally eradicates a sense that music-drama lacks musical form. The second Act is literally a symphony, with all the tension and self-contained unity of symphonic form, and yet it is also so much an opera at this moment that the listener who does not know otherwise will not even think of a symphony.

It is by no means pointless, especially today, to remind ourselves that *Wozzeck* is an opera and that Berg described it as such. Music written for today's opera houses tends increasingly to be incidental music of a cinematic nature, or more suited to radio plays and mere background music. In *Wozzeck*, by contrast, where the music completely absorbs the text, the music is the main point of interest and it ought to be the focus of attention both in performance and when we listen to the score. With an utterly sure instinct

Berg the avant-garde composer demanded a 'realistic' staging, so that attention should not be diverted from the music. The score is thematic, expounding graphic motifs or themes in every scene, transforming them and giving them a history. It also demands to be played thematically, above all so that the musical characters are absolutely recognisable and thrown into sharp relief. The themes and their development must be followed in detail, whether they be those of the jewelry scene, which is derived, sonata-like, from the tiniest motifs, or the Scherzo which constitutes the long inn scene, or the transformations of the variations on a theme in Marie's Bible scene, where the theme is boldly assembled from a tonality appropriate to biblical style and outbursts of atonality. In spite of Berg's imaginative use of tonal colour, in spite of such striking orchestral effects as the B that increases in volume to breaking-point after Marie's death or the ripples on the pond's surface as Wozzeck drowns — the sound is always secondary, the result of purely musico-thematic events and produced by them alone.

If one concentrates on these musical events as one would, for example, on the melodies of a traditional opera, everything else will become clear of its own accord, including the mood that typifies Berg: the paralysing fear in the scene in the open field, the off-stage march — both strident and sombre — and the lullaby as an echo of Nature which, though suppressed, breaks out in song; the ineffable melancholy of the Ländler in the inn scene, Wozzeck's dark question about time, and his disturbed sleep in the barracks scene. The alien quality of popular music, the wretched stunted happiness of serving-girls and soldiers, is heard by Berg and given full compositional treatment, not with Stravinskian mockery but with the expressive gentleness of boundless compassion. His dramatic imagination so strongly extends the techniques of composition that he anticipates much that was not to be written for thirty years: one thinks, for example, of the way he includes rhythm in the art of thematic variation, which was then rediscovered in serial music — the quick and brutal piano polka in the opening bars of the second tavern scene provides the rhythmic model for everything that then races past us in this scene. So perfect is the work that all it demands is attentive readiness to receive what it gives in profligate abundance. The listener should not shy away from a love which unreservedly seeks out human beings where they are most in need.

This article is reproduced by permission of Verlag Elisabeth Lafite, Vienna; Österreichischer Bundesverlag für Unterricht, Wissenschaft und Kunst, Vienna, 1968.

'Wozzeck' at Covent Garden

These impressions and letters appeared in 'The Musical Times' after the first London staging of 'Wozzeck', at Covent Garden in 1952.

March, 1952

By giving us *Wozzeck*, the largest but one of our operatic arrears, the Covent Garden management has earned a credit that outweighs half-a-dozen failures. The thing was done handsomely. First place to Erich Kleiber (who conducted the first performance of the work, at Berlin in 1925); no score of like modernism has been played to us with such intimacy, such fine grading and moulding, and such vibrant feeling. Throughout the evening the musical listener was confronted with beauty, and it was through this screen that he beheld the sordid drama on the stage. To one observer it was as if the characters were living their life under compulsion of that intense, dominating music in the orchestra. The scenery by Caspar Neher was effective, unassertive (none of your cheap surrealism here), and individual enough to set up a challenge to other settings. Some of these settings are illustrated in the January issue of that excellent periodical *Opera*. In the face of these samples from Philadelphia in 1931, Rome in 1942 and Berne in 1951, we may be thankful that Neher's departures from realism went no further than an interior without ceiling or roof. No doubt this was for the benefit of the scene-shifters, who performed miracles in getting twelve of the fifteen scenes ready in time. Next, Sumner Austin as producer: a happy choice, for the stage work showed the hand of experience in its naturalness and smooth operation. There were two casts — a further mark of thoroughness. The principals were the following (those of the second cast in brackets); Wozzeck, Marko Rothmüller (Jess Walters); Captain, Parry Jones (Max Worthley); Doctor, Frederick Dalberg (Otakar Kraus); Drum Major, Thorsteinn Hannesson (Frank Sale); Marie, Christel Goltz. The first-night cast, on January 22, was never less than competent, and in Rothmüller it had a Wozzeck of whom only one criticism has been made — that he seemed at times to be the most intelligent person on the stage. (Indeed, give him a smirk, and he might have been Good Soldier Schweik himself.) The casting of the Captain and the Doctor served to point a criticism of the opera in one of its aspects. Although Parry Jones and Dalberg played their parts well, as dramatic figures they seemed hardly sinister and potent enough to be the agents of a man's destruction. Added together they were less formidable than the malign Claggart of *Billy Budd*. We refrain from further critical remarks since the field is sufficiently covered by the five personal impressions that now follow.

Thoughts on 'Wozzeck'

'You and your critical brood have been clamouring for *Wozzeck* for a long time. Now that you've got it I hope you're satisfied.' I mumbled some appreciative words to the speaker, who was a member of the Covent Garden staff. I felt strongly that this much-criticized opera company had shown that it could behave in a thoroughly adult manner in carrying through such a difficult work with conspicuous success.

But 'satisfied'? No. In the first place, quite physically, so far from being satisfied, I felt as though I had lost about a quart of blood. *Wozzeck* is immensely lowering to the spirit without having the cleansing quality of catharsis. Should great art be lowering? I say no: even the darkest tragedy should have its ethos, its power to uplift and to edify the mind. If a work of art has this quality, then one can experience it again and again. But after two viewings of the opera, another two hearings and an un*Times*ley study of the score, I don't want to undergo *Wozzeck* again for a decade or two. I do not care for the subjective quality of so much of Berg's music. I don't want my emotions dragged through the sink and the gutter. Berg's music deals with such a subject too thoroughly, too inclusively. Everything is written in the score and everything in art is too much. There's nothing left to the imagination, nothing left for the singer to act. (Perhaps this is due to the Schönberg group's fear of being 'interpreted', which also leads them to issue explicit instructions for the performance of each note and even, in *Wozzeck*, each silent pause.) And there is precious little to sing, so that the actor is left standing on the stage like a puppet with the orchestra working overtime: in this respect Berg is Wagner to the *n*th degree.

Perhaps I should say now, in order to prevent my assassination by — never mind whom — that in spite of all this I cannot avoid conceding the word masterpiece to *Wozzeck*. Here is the most intensely emotional music bridled by a most masterly brain. Nothing else in this century has produced quite such an overwhelming impression. *Wozzeck* has an effect on us belonging to our day and to our time that it cannot have on anybody else in any much later time. Just in the way that *Tristan*, however strongly it may hit us nowadays if we hear it for the first time, cannot make the same impression as it did in the latter half of the nineteenth century. The shock-tactics of *Tristan* have become common knowledge even before we see it. The musical language of *Wozzeck* is not yet common currency, though some of the more advanced American bands, like that of Stan Kenton, are approaching Berg's harmonic idiom.

To sum up: emotionally *Wozzeck* is as much a dead-end as Delius: in matters of technique and the intellect it will remain an important work; a fascinating and beautiful *fleur du mal*.

John Amis

The Character of Wozzeck

The character of Wozzeck, both in Georg Büchner's original drama *Woyzeck* and in the operatic adaptation made by Alban Berg, is of considerable interest. Those who speak of him as a half-wit or a dumb ox are wide of the mark. He shows many of the characteristics of the Slav temperament. He is slow to move: yet he feels deeply. He accepts unquestioningly the necessity of suffering. 'I am a simple soul. Folk like us are always unfortunate — in this world and in any other world.' He finds difficulty in expressing himself; and this is particularly frustrating, for he is a visionary. He sees the sunset with all the intensity of an expressionist painter like Vincent Van Gogh. 'A fire! A fire there! It rises from earth into heaven, and with a tumult falling, just like trumpets.' His senses pierce the outward mask. Beneath the grass of the field he hears the sinister rumour of a separate life. When he identifies this mysterious underground movement with the Freemasons he is as convinced as William Blake was in identifying his spiritual visitants with the Man who built the Pyramids, or Wat Tyler, or the Ghost of a Flea. But Wozzeck unfortunately is not blessed with the artist's capacity of freeing himself from an obsession by expressing it through his art. Instead, he becomes giddy as he sees the ground quaking and the precipice opening at his feet.

In his need to earn more than his bare private's pay in order to keep his mistress Marie and their illegitimate child, he is forced to undertake odd jobs such as serving as the Captain's batman. But it is with a touch of horror that one finds him lending himself as a subject for the Doctor's dietetic experiments. The Doctor treats him as a human guinea-pig and does not scruple to tamper with the delicate mechanism of his will-power.

To delineate the tragedy of Wozzeck, Berg has to show him as a man who is at once an ordinary poor soldier and also a visionary who has:

Known panic and the fisted fear that knocks
By marsh, moor and grey meadow.

It is the essence of his tragedy that circumstances make it impossible for him to integrate the different parts of his split personality. Berg's musical idiom with its distorted harmonic structure is wonderfully well adapted for this purpose. The effect is heightened by the abnormal tension caused by the excessively disciplined form of the score as related to the simple episodic character of the drama.

The Slav temperament does not change quickly; and many of Wozzeck's qualities are characteristic of the Slav today. The German Captain and Doctor signally failed to understand him in Büchner's play — so did Marie. Would the Germans — or the Western Europeans for that matter — be more likely to understand and sympathize today? At a time when the personality of Europe is split in two by the shadow of a curtain, it is particularly fortunate that Berg has seen the true nature of Wozzeck's tragedy and given it immortal expression and universal currency in operatic form.

Eric Walter White

Marko Rothmüller (Wozzeck) and Christel Goltz (Marie), Covent Garden, 1952 (photo: Angus McBean © Harvard Theatre Collection)

43

An Expectation Fulfilled

No doubt it was unwise to come to *Wozzeck* with as high an expectation as I had. So often one is disappointed when looking forward not merely to hearing a performance, but to re-living or intensifying a previous experience. I had been profoundly moved by a concert performance of this opera — not the BBC's performance of two years ago, which stands with somewhat uncertain outlines in my memory, but that given in New York under Dimitri Mitropoulos only ten months since. I had felt then not only the power of the individual sections of the opera, but the cogency of its dramatic shape. Now I was to see this shape realized in a stage presentation.

I was not disappointed. The settings and the visual characterization — despite certain shortcomings, for instance in the Drum Major — alike helped to heighten the experience of the music. The division into as many as fifteen scenes did not give the effect of fragmentation: rather the effect was that of a moving-picture camera, picking up the story now from a new angle, now returning to an old one. Caspar Neher's settings admirably preserved this unity, though the basis of the unity lies in the music itself. Even those parts of the score most striking in themselves seem to gain by their theatrical setting. Take, for instance, the stupendous *crescendo* for the whole orchestra on the single note B (after the death of Marie), building up a tension which suddenly collapses as the out-of-tune piano starts the wild polka on a distorted chord of C major. How much is added by the fact that the *crescendo* takes place in the darkened theatre, with the curtain down, and that the piano's entry coincides with the raising of the curtain on the populated interior of the shabbily-lit tavern!

The most vividly realized of the characters, to my mind, was the Captain of Parry Jones. The most unexpected characterization was provided by Christel Goltz. She was not the dull, almost uncomprehending Marie one had imagined, but something active and sensual. Yet her characterization 'came off', rising to true pathos in the Bible-reading scene. Perhaps, indeed, the 'active' aspect of this Marie made for a better total balance of this opera, in which so many of the characters are mere rollers for Fate's wheel. At any rate, nothing marred my impression that I was undergoing one of the major operatic experiences of my life.

Arthur Jacobs

A Great Operatic Experience

There are a number of paradoxical features about *Wozzeck*. Being a real opera, it needs the stage to make its full impact; but the greater part of that impact emerges from the orchestra. It is a drama of low life, hallucination and sordidness, yet over the whole work hovers an aura of nobility. Büchner's play was written in 1837 but breathes the same air as the Doctors Caligari and Mabuse: Berg's music was written between 1914 and 1921, but its climate has nothing to do with time or period. And yet the collaboration of the two artists is as close as any in the history of opera, a history rich in successful collaborations.

The tonal climate again is peculiar. Only two passages, Marie's fairy tale and the last interlude, are 'in' a key with attendant key-signatures, and a few more, such as Margret's Schwabenland number and the Ländler in Act Two, inhabit a tonally stable atmosphere; elsewhere common chords and chords with key-implications are used, but not often with particular reference to a prevailing tonality. What is peculiar is that an anchorage is nearly always to be felt; and yet people still refer to *Wozzeck* as an atonal opera; it is of course

44

wrong to call it a twelve-note opera, when Berg made no effort to employ the method systematically, for the simple reason that Schönberg had not then formulated his Method of Composition.

In the end, tonal and historical climates, morality, balance of power and form are beguiling but not really important; as Berg pointed out, the impact of the drama upon the emotions, which goes further than the fate of one individual, is what counts. At Covent Garden on January 22, that impact was felt, despite some weaknesses in casting, decor and production. Marko Rothmüller's portrayal of Wozzeck, as a great mind *manqué* through nobody's fault but nature's, and destroyed by human blindness and selfishness, commanded the stage at every turn. Berg's music, which for most of the time means what goes on in the pit, was superbly served by Erich Kleiber. *Wozzeck* cannot fail to dumbfound a listener susceptible to the Viennese tradition in music. These two contributions made sure that people like me, who are thus susceptible and who had not seen *Wozzeck* in the theatre before, will remember that performance as one of the great operatic experiences of their lives.

W.S. Mann

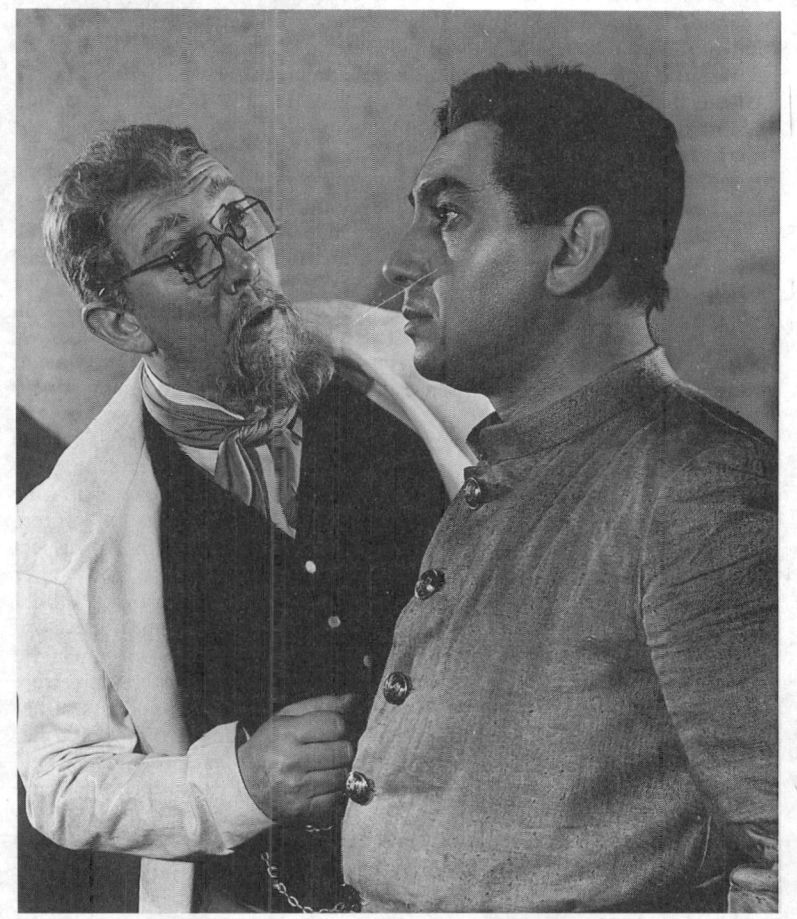

Frederick Dalberg (Doctor) and Marko Rothmüller (Wozzeck), Covent Garden 1952 (photo: Angus McBean © Harvard Theatre Collection)

A Reflection Prompted by the Second Cast

Dr Kleiber's handling of the eloquent orchestral score of *Wozzeck* won universal praise; the singers, too, put up a brave show in view of their inexperience with music of this for-the-most-part keyless kind requiring *Sprechstimme* as well as *Gesangstimme*. Why, then, was it that the performance undertaken by the second cast on February 5 gripped and fascinated without rousing in the spectator that profound sense of compassion which prompted first Büchner and later Berg to immortalize the barber, Woyzeck, executed in the Market Square of Leipzig in the presence of a large crowd on August 27, 1824? (For simplicity let us call him Wozzeck, the name adopted by Berg.)

It is pertinent to recall that before the execution took place, a court of inquiry was set up under Hofrat Dr Clarus to ascertain whether or not Wozzeck was mad. Every producer of the opera should do something of the same kind. The original Wozzeck had suffered in earlier life from occasional epileptic fits, he was known to have had a persecution mania (thinking the Freemasons were after him), and he was adjudged to be morally depraved. But there was no evidence that he was mad. In the play, there is overwhelming evidence that the Wozzeck created by Büchner was neither mad nor morally depraved. Admittedly he had 'toadstool' hallucinations as well as Freemasons on his mind; but no one knew better than Büchner, as the son of a doctor and a medical student himself, that little is more likely to cause hallucinations than malnutrition — that is, the prolonged diet of beans enforced on Wozzeck, for experimental purposes, by the Doctor. Why did Wozzeck endure this guinea-pigging, it may be asked, if he was fundamentally in his right mind? The answer is to earn a few extra pence to alleviate the poverty of Marie, whom he genuinely loved. In his own words to the Doctor: 'I need this money for my wife. That is why I'm here.' Further examination of Büchner's text reveals that although, as a result of the Doctor's experiments, Wozzeck was a sick man, and moreover a man who acted always by instinct rather than by reason, he was by no means the idiot that Mr Jess Walters made him on February 5. How can we feel for a Wozzeck who is too sub-human even to be capable of experiencing a dumb animal's sense of right and wrong, and capacity for affection and suffering?

Characterization is scarcely less important in Marie's case. There is absolutely nothing in common between Frau Woost, the widow and 'amateur prostitute, with a special penchant for soldiers' murdered by Wozzeck in June 1821 and Büchner's Marie, who is weak, admittedly, but not a wanton. Büchner's Marie has no physical desire for the Drum Major; in this respect her own resigned words 'Have your way, then. It is all the same' after abandoning her struggle with him are far more significant than the earlier remark of a catty neighbour, 'everyone knows that *you* can't keep your eyes off any man'. In her life of unrelieved, grey poverty and drabness, his splendid appearance, gifts of ear-rings and invitations to the gay tavern gardens were the fundamental cause of her acquiescence. And of the genuineness of her remorse Büchner gives a striking instance in each of the two scenes in her room. Christel Goltz, though musically confident and vivacious, must be held responsible for alienating our sympathies still further by transforming Marie into little less than a harlot.

But there are two characters who must at all costs be shown in their worst possible light — one is the Doctor, and the other the Captain. The Doctor we know to have been a caricature of Büchner's particular bête-noir, Wilbrand, crack-pot professor of anatomy at Giessen University, and it is by no means over-fanciful to suggest that Berg, who experienced military life himself in 1914-18, had no affection for the Captain when portraying him musically. The

Frederick Dalberg (Doctor), Marko Rothmüller (Wozzeck) and Parry Jones (Captain), Covent Garden, 1952 (photo: Angus McBean © Harvard Theatre Collection)

Captain's moral worth is proved once and for all when after continuously taunting Wozzeck, he breaks down like a child (though far more foolishly) on being told by the Doctor of an approaching 'apoplexia cerebri'. The Doctor, however, is little short of a criminal lunatic, for his experiments with diet are dangerous enough to be held responsible for Wozzeck's ultimate inability to resist the temptation of the 'knife-blade'. His obsession (brilliantly depicted by Berg by means of a passacaglia) with the idea of fame and immortality blind him to all sense of moral responsibility. Otakar Kraus went a little further than his predecessor Frederick Dalberg, in suggesting the sinister implications of the part, and Max Worthley was certainly more foolish than Parry Jones as the Captain. But neither pair went nearly far enough away from harmless comedy towards a suggestion of the malevolent powers against which Wozzeck and Marie were pitted.

The smaller parts are less important. But it would be no exaggeration to claim that the four principals have a greater responsibility as interpreters in *Wozzeck* than in any other opera. Unless the spectator can take Wozzeck and Marie to his heart, as much for their own sakes as for the forces which seek to destroy them, there can be no feeling of escape from the particular to the universal — no sharing with Berg of that overwhelming sense of pity for the weak and oppressed that is told to us as much in that last great D minor interlude as by the unforgettable expression on the composer's sensitive face.

Joan Chissell

Letters to the Editor

May, 1952

May I be permitted to rush in where your five critics of *Wozzeck* feared to tread? I have reluctantly come to the conclusion that the work is a failure, and that the blame must be laid firmly on the shoulders of Berg the librettist and Berg the composer.

The fundamental weakness is a dramatic one. You cannot have black without white, or darkness without light; yet Berg attempts to portray insanity without any reference to sanity itself. All the major characters are abnormal; none are sympathetic. Moreover, there is a complete lack of dramatic development. Wozzeck's mania is already apparent in the very first Act; there is no growth of character, but simply a sequence of depressing events. Consequently the climax is merely sensational, not truly dramatic.

This weakness is paralleled by a similar lack of growth in the music. In the wood-cutting scene in Act One Berg is already using the full range of dissonance and orchestral *fortissimo*; by the time we reach the dénouement the ear is wearied and even the famous D minor adagio loses much of its impact. A good example of this loss of power can be found in the scene in the Doctor's surgery. Ernest Newman tells us (in *Opera Nights*) that as the Doctor reaches the word 'immortal' — 'his vocal line becomes more and more extravagantly absurd, till his megalomania culminates in a crazy trill'. Here, as elsewhere, the listener has no sense of culmination whatever, because the vocal line has been crazy from the very beginning.

Admirers of *Wozzeck* point to the many beautiful and novel sonorities revealed in the orchestral score. But sonorities by themselves are not enough; the musical thought expressed through those sonorities must be sound, if the value of the work is to remain after the actual novelty has worn off. They also explain away Berg's rejection of normal dramatic procedures by describing the opera as a fantasy or nightmare, subject only to the irrational logic of the world of dreams. If this is true, it would certainly account for much of the tedium of the work; for in the whole range of human experience there are few ordeals more boring than being subjected to a lengthy recitation of other people's dreams.

This is not to deny that there are fine moments in the work. It is significant that in the finest — the orchestral prelude to the final scene — Berg returns to tonality, and it is also significant that it was conceived, as Newman tells us, independently of the actual opera. Even in his finest moments, however, it is questionable whether Berg adds anything, apart from technique, to what other Romantic composers have written before him. As Cecil Gray puts it in his essay 'Contingencies': 'It is probably the chief flaw in Berg as an artist, in fact, that he so often seems to employ a new technique and vocabulary in order to achieve what can be achieved, and has already been achieved, by simpler and more orthodox means.'

How then can I explain the enthusiasm with which the work has been received, and the statement that for two of your critics it has been one of the major artistic experiences of their lives? Some listeners undoubtedly are in sympathy with Berg's outlook and are genuinely moved by his music. But I can't help feeling that the majority are impressed only *because they feel they ought to be*. Since genius has in the past been occasionally allied to obscurity, they have come to believe that obscurity is *ipso facto* a proof of genius. They have been told so often by Superior Persons that *Wozzeck* is a masterpiece that they no longer have the courage to disagree. In short, the chorus of praise for Berg's opera reminds one irresistibly of the applause for the Emperor's New Clothes which greeted him as he appeared stark naked on the balcony of his palace.

Geoffrey Bush

[As the result of seeing the 1960 production of the opera at Covent Garden *sung in English*, Geoffrey Bush came round to the belief that *Wozzeck*, though flawed — like *Fidelio* — was nevertheless a masterpiece.]

Christel Goltz as Marie, Covent Garden, 1952 (photo: Angus McBean © Harvard Theatre Collection)

David Tree (The Idiot) and Jess Walters (Wozzeck), Covent Garden, 1952 (photo: Angus McBean © Harvard Theatre Collection)

As one who regards Berg's *Wozzeck* as an unqualified masterpiece, I would be the last to deny that there is an arguable case against the work on aesthetic grounds; but I feel that Dr Geoffrey Bush's letter in the May *Musical Times* can only obscure the issue by its misconception of the intention of the opera and its disregard for demonstrable fact. His flat statement that *Wozzeck* portrays insanity without reference to sanity itself, and that all the main characters are abnormal, is incorrect: Marie and the Drum Major are familiar, normal types, to be met at any time in the vicinity of an army barracks, and Wozzeck behaves like a normal private soldier most of the time, his occasional hallucinations being clearly marked off from his normal state, dramatically and musically. In any case, the opera is not a portrayal of insanity, but a representation of the misery of the pitiable dregs of human civilization, built round a straightforward central plot of a woman's unfaithfulness, a man's jealousy, and a resultant *crime passionel*.

It is quite untrue to say that there is neither dramatic development nor growth of character. Wozzeck's character develops from simple faith in Marie, through realization of her unfaithfulness, to jealousy and the desire to kill her; and her character develops from pity and affection for Wozzeck, through her unfaithfulness, to defiance of him, and later, bitter remorse. In consequence, the climax (her death) is truly dramatic, in that it is brought about by the interaction of these motives.

To find *none* of the characters sympathetic is to lay oneself open to the charge of lack of heart, or lack of understanding: surely Wozzeck's defence of his illegitimate child and his prayer not to be led into temptation, and Marie's love for the child and her remorse for her sin, not to mention the actual sins of both, bear witness to their essential humanity, and awake a response in any feeling person.

To impute lack of growth to the music is to confess ignorance of the score, which proceeds from the simplest of textures through an increasingly complex contrapuntal web of leading motifs to culminate in the well-known summing-up in D minor. The statement that Berg reached the full range of dissonance and orchestral *fortissimo* as early as the second scene (which is not true with regard to dissonance) proves nothing; the texture is still simple compared with the later complexities of the score. The particular case of the Doctor's scene, mentioned by Dr Bush, is an admirable example of the cumulative effect of the music: the vocal line begins quietly in perfectly normal speech-rhythm recitative over the passacaglia bass alone, becoming 'extravagantly absurd' only in the last two or three variations.

As for Cecil Gray's remark that Berg employed a new technique and vocabulary to achieve what can be achieved, and has been achieved, by simpler and more orthodox means, surely no one can take it seriously? It is impossible to imagine a *Wozzeck* by Wagner or Richard Strauss that would have had the same kind of impact as Berg's has.

If we are to continue arguing about *Wozzeck*, let us at least be fair, and admit that it is a realistic opera, with a story that can be read daily in the papers, and characters that one may find oneself sitting next to on the bus; that the drama is well-constructed, and the plot logical and inevitable; and that the music is a masterly hammering-home of the dreadful implications of the drama. After this, those who find such a vivid representation of a certain aspect of reality repugnant to their tastes are entitled to say, if they wish, that art should not concern itself with such things, and that therefore they have no place on the operatic stage. This is an aesthetic question which may be argued at length.

One last word: if one cannot understand a work of art, and has not the patience to study it in detail, the easiest way out is to 'reluctantly' consider it a failure, to label it 'obscure', to accuse those who *do* understand it of being 'superior persons', and to conclude that lesser mortals who admire it are guilty of snobbism. *Wozzeck* itself is perfectly clear; the obscurity is in Dr Bush's mind.

Deryck Cooke

August, 1952

Heartily though I sympathized with Dr Bush's attack on *Wozzeck*, it seems to me that he missed the main charge against the opera and thereby exposed himself to Mr Deryck Cooke's effective rejoinder in your last month's issue. As I see it, the main charge is not that the libretto is not dramatic, or that the music lacks structural 'development', but that it expresses an almost uniform *revulsion* towards the events it illustrates. This is a pity, in the first place because, as Mr Cooke says, 'Marie and the Drum Major are familiar, normal types, to be met at any time in the vicinity of an army barracks', whose behaviour by no means merits the appalling avalanche of discord which it evokes, and in the second place because revulsion, even if continuously justified, is not an emotion capable of sustaining a whole evening's drama, however 'realistic'. A one-act 'shocker' perhaps; but a full-length opera purporting to offer a serious comment on 'Life' surely must express a *range* of feeling. *Wozzeck*, for all the skill and forcefulness of the music, gives the inpression of being merely the product of a disturbed mind, of an artist unable to measure and master his chosen subject-matter.

Robert L. Jacobs

Christel Goltz (Marie) and Marko Rothmüller (Wozzeck), Covent Garden, 1952 (photo: Royal Opera House Archives)

Thematic Guide

Many of the themes from *Wozzeck* have been identified in the articles by numbers in square brackets, which refer to the themes set out in these pages. The themes are also identified by the numbers in square brackets at the corresponding points in the libretto, so that the words can be related to the musical themes.

[1] CAPTAIN

[2] 'POOR FOLK LIKE US!'

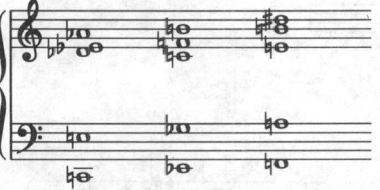

Wir ar – me Leut'!   Sehn Sie,   Herr Haupt–mann,...
Poor folk like us!   Mo – ney.   you see Sir,

[3]

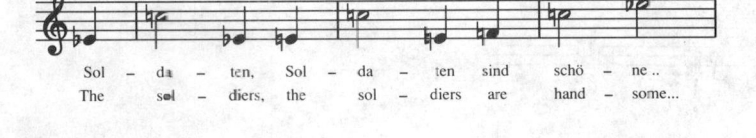

[4] MARCH

Sol – da – ten, Sol – da – ten sind schö – ne ..
The sol – diers, the sol – diers are hand – some...

[5] MARIE

[6] LULLABY

[7] 'DEATH'

[8] DOCTOR

[9] 'SEDUCTION MUSIC'

[10] FIGHT MUSIC

[11]

[12] WOZZECK

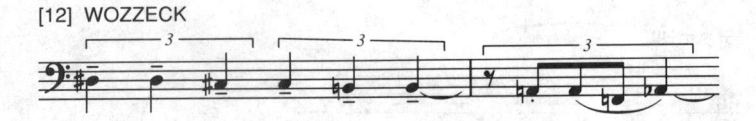

[13] KNIFE

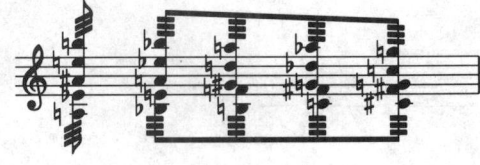

54

Evelyne Lear as Marie, San Francisco Opera, 1968 (photo: Carolyn Mason Jones)

Top: Act One, scene three (Marie's room); centre: Act Two, scene four (tavern garden) and below: Act Three, scene four (Forest path by the pool), in the Metropolitan Opera sets designed by Caspar Neher; Herbert Graf's production revived by David Alden, 1989 (photos: Winnie Klotz)

Wozzeck

Opera in Three Acts (Fifteen Scenes) by Alban Berg
Text by Alban Berg after *Woyzeck* by Georg Büchner

The opera is dedicated to Alma Maria Mahler.

English translation by Eric Blackall and Vida Harford

The first performance of *Wozzeck* was at the Berlin Staatsoper on December 14, 1925. The first performance in the United States was in Philadelphia on March 19, 1931. The first performance in Britain was in concert form, at the Queen's Hall, London, on March 14, 1934. The first British stage production was at the Royal Opera House, Covent Garden on January 22, 1952.

This English text is a performing translation of the opera, made originally for the Covent Garden première in 1952, and substantially revised for later productions. It is set out against the full text of the Franzos/Landau edition of Büchner's play, which was the basis for Berg's libretto. All the scenes, phrases and words of the play which were not incorporated into the libretto are given, either in square brackets or footnotes; where complete scenes were omitted, they are included in the sequence with a headnote to that effect. The translations of these passages have been made especially for this Guide by Stewart Spencer, and obviously form no part of the Harford/ Blackall translation of the libretto. German spellings follow the Berg text for the libretto and the idiosyncratic Franzos spellings for the play.

The Act and scene divisions follow those of the libretto (there is no definitive sequence for Büchner's play, and so the play scenes are not numbered), and a table showing how the two relate is given on the next page. Since the Franzos/Landau edition, Büchner research has identified different readings and additional material which are not included in this Guide. The stage directions are those of the opera.

'Wozzeck' and 'Woyzeck': a list of scenes

'Wozzeck' the opera libretto by Berg

'Woyzeck' the play by Büchner, edited by Franzos and Landau

ACT ONE

Scene One
The Captain's room

A room
Woyzeck shaves the Captain

Scene Two
Open fields. The town in the distance. Late afternoon.

Open fields. The town in the distance
Woyzeck and Andres cut sticks.

Scene Three
Marie's room. Evening

The town
Marie watches the military band. She sings to the child. Woyzeck visits.

Scene Four
The Doctor's study. A sunny afternoon

The Doctor's study
The Doctor examines Woyzeck.

—

An open place. Booths
Marie and Woyzeck go to the fair.

—

In one of the booths
Marie and Woyzeck watch a performing donkey.

Scene Five
Street before Marie's dwelling. Evening twilight.

Street
The Drum Major seduces Marie.

ACT TWO

Scene One
Marie's room. Morning, sunshine

Room
Marie admires the earrings. Woyzeck discovers her.

Scene Two
Street. Day

Street
The Doctor and the Captain taunt Woyzeck

Scene Three
Street before Marie's dwelling. Dull day

Marie's room
Woyzeck confronts Marie.

—

Guard room
Woyzeck and Andres

Scene Four
Tavern garden. Late evening

Tavern
Woyzeck watches Marie dance with the Drum Major. He is approached by the idiot.

—

Open country. Night
Woyzeck hears voices and music.

Scene Five
A guardroom in the barracks. Night

—

ACT THREE
Scene One
Marie's room. Night. Candlelight.

—

(The fairy tale is incorporated into the previous scene.)

—

Scene Two
A forest path by a pool. Twilight

Scene Three
A low tavern. Night. Dimly lit

Scene Four
The forest path by the pool. Moonlit night as before

Scene Five
In front of Marie's dwelling. Bright morning sunshine.

—

Barracks. Night
Unable to sleep, Woyzeck wakes Andres

The barracks yard
The Drum Major taunts and fights Woyzeck.

Marie's room
Marie reads the Bible.

Junk shop
Woyzeck buys the knife.

Street. Sunday afternoon
Marie watches the children playing. An old woman tells a fairy story.

Barracks
Woyzeck gives his coat to Andres.

A forest path by a pool. Twilight
Woyzeck murders Marie

A low tavern
Woyzeck tries to get drunk

A forest path by the pool. Night
Woyzeck drowns.

In front of Marie's dwelling. Early morning
The children play.

Dissecting room
A doctor and a judge comment on the murder.

CHARACTERS

Wozzeck	Wozzeck	*baritone and speaking voice*
Drum Major	Tambourmajor	*heroic tenor*
Andres	Andres	*lyric tenor and speaking voice*
Captain	Hauptmann	*buffo tenor*
Doctor	Doktor	*buffo bass*
First Apprentice	1. Handwerksbursch	*deep bass and speaking voice*
Second Apprentice	2. Handwerksbursch	*high baritone (possibly tenor)*
The Idiot	Der Narr	*high tenor*
Marie	Marie	*soprano*
Margret	Margret	*contralto*
Marie's son	Mariens Knabe	*if possible, singing voice (Act Three, scene five)*
Soldiers and Apprentices	Soldaten und Burschen	*tenor I and II baritone I and II bass I and II*
a Soldier from amongst them	davon ein Soldat	*solo tenor (Act Two, scene five and Act Three, scene three)*
Serving Girls and Young Women	Mägde und Dirnen	*sopranos and contraltos in two parts unison*
Children	Kinder	*in unison*

Act One

Scene One. *The Captain's room. Early in the morning. The Captain is sitting on a chair in front of a mirror. Wozzeck is shaving the Captain.* [1]

CAPTAIN

Slowly, Wozzeck, slowly! Do take your time, man!

anxiously

You make me quite giddy ...

He covers his forehead and eyes with his hand, and steadies himself. Wozzeck stops working.

What can I do with the ten minutes that you save me if you finish early today?

Wozzeck continues shaving.

more vigorously

Wozzeck, consider, you surely still have almost thirty years to live yet! Thirty years; that's three hundred and sixty months, you know, and how many days and hours and minutes! What will you do with the great expanse of time before you now?

serious again

Sort yourself out, Wozzeck!

WOZZECK

Yes, Sir. Quite so, Sir!

CAPTAIN
confidingly

It makes me afraid for the world, to think of eternity. [Work, Wozzeck, work!] 'Eternal', that's for ever! (You understand.) But then again, it cannot be for ever, but a mere moment, yes, a moment! Wozzeck, I shudder when I think that the whole world revolves in a single day: [What a waste! — What's the point of it all? Everything goes so quickly! – Wozzeck] and if I see a mill-wheel that turns, it always gives me melancholia!

WOZZECK

Quite so, Sir!

CAPTAIN

Wozzeck, you always look so harassed! A worthy man doesn't act like that. A worthy man, with a conscience that's worthy, does things slowly ....
Do say something, Wozzeck. Come tell me, how's the weather?

WOZZECK

It's bad, it's bad, Captain! [Bad.] Wind!

Langsam, Wozzeck, langsam! Eins nach dem Andern!

Er macht mir ganz schwindlich ...

Was soll ich denn mit den zehn Minuten anfangen, die Er heut' zu früh fertig wird?

Wozzeck, bedenk' Er, Er hat noch seine schönen dreissig Jahr' zu leben! Dreissig Jahre macht dreihundert und sechzig Monate und erst wieviel Tage, Stunden, Minuten! Was will Er denn mit der ungeheuren Zeit all anfangen?

Teil' Er sich ein, Wozzeck!

[1] Jawohl, Herr Hauptmann!

Es wird mir ganz angst um die Welt, wenn ich an die Ewigkeit denk'. [Beschäftigung, Wozzeck, Beschäftigung!] 'Ewig', das ist ewig! (das sieht Er ein.) Nun ist es aber wieder nicht ewig, sondern[1] ein Augenblick, ja, ein Augenblick! Wozzeck, es schaudert mich, wenn ich denke, dass sich die Welt in einem Tag herumdreht: [Was für eine Zeitverschwendung! — Wo soll das hinaus? So geschwind geht alles! — Wozzeck] drum kann ich auch kein Mühlrad mehr sehn, oder ich werde melancholisch!

Jawohl, Herr Hauptmann!

Wozzeck, Er sieht immer so verhetzt aus! Ein guter Mensch tut das nicht. Ein guter Mensch, der sein gutes Gewissen hat, tut alles langsam ....
Red' Er doch was, Wozzeck. Was ist heut für ein[2] Wetter?

Sehr[3] schlimm, Herr Hauptmann! [schlimm.] Wind!

---

1. das ist ein Augenblick   2. für Wetter   3. Schlimm, Herr Hauptmann!

CAPTAIN

I feel it, there's something so swift
outside there; such a wind always seems
to me just like a mouse.

artfully

I think that it is blowing from South-
North?

WOZZECK

Yes, Sir. Quite so, Sir.

CAPTAIN
laughing loudly

South-North!

He laughs still more loudly.

Oh, you are dense, quite absurdly dense!

sympathetically

Wozzeck, you are a worthy man,

striking an attitude

and yet [Wozzeck]

like a fanfare

you possess no morality!

very dignified

Morality: that's behaving morally! (Is
that clear? It is a splendid word.)

very grandly

You have a child which is not blessed by
the clergy! . . .

WOZZECK

Yes, Sir . . .

He stops.

CAPTAIN

. . . As our regimental chaplain says to
us when he preaches: 'which is not
blessed by the clergy' — (The words are
not my own.)

WOZZECK

But Captain, the good Lord God will
not spurn the poor little mite just
because the Amen was not spoken
before a child was made. The Lord
spake: 'Suffer the children to come to
me!'

CAPTAIN
jumping up in a rage

What does he mean? And what sort of
curious answer is that? You make me
quite confused [with your answer]!

His voice cracks.

When I say 'he', then I mean 'you',
'you' . . .

WOZZECK

Poor folk like us! Money, you see, Sir,
money! With no money . . . Let one of

CAPTAIN

Ich spür's schon, 's ist so was
Geschwindes draussen; so ein Wind
macht mir den Effekt, wie eine Maus.

Ich glaub, wir haben so was aus Süd-
Nord?

WOZZECK

Jawohl, Herr Hauptmann.

CAPTAIN

Süd-Nord!

Oh, Er ist dumm, ganz abscheulich
dumm!

Wozzeck, Er ist ein guter Mensch,

aber [Wozzeck] . . .

Er hat keine Moral!

Moral: das ist, wenn man moralisch ist!
(Versteht Er? Es ist ein gutes Wort.)

Er hat ein Kind ohne den Segen der
Kirche! . . .

WOZZECK

Jawo . . .[1]

CAPTAIN

. . . wie unser hochwürdiger Herr
Garnisonsprediger sagt: 'Ohne den
Segen der Kirche' — (Das Wort ist
nicht von mir.)

WOZZECK

Herr Hauptmann, der liebe Gott wird
den armen Wurm nicht drum ansehn,
ob das Amen darüber gesagt ist, eh er
gemacht wurde. Der Herr sprach:
'Lasset die Kleinen zu mir kommen!'

CAPTAIN

Was sagt Er da?! Was ist das für eine
kuriose Antwort? Er macht mich ganz
konfus [mit seiner Antwort]!

Wenn ich sage: 'Er', so mein ich 'Ihn',
'Ihn' . . .

WOZZECK

[2] Wir arme Leut! Sehn Sie, Herr
Hauptmann, Geld, Geld! Wer kein Geld

---

1. Berg's interpolation

us try to bring his own kind into the world, in a good moral way! We're all made of flesh and blood! If I were a gentleman, Sir, and wore a top hat, and had a watch, and an eyeglass too, and could talk politely, then I would be virtuous, too! It must be beautiful to have virtue, my Captain. But I'm only a simple soul. Folk like us always are unfortunate in this world and the other world! I think that if we got into heaven, we'd have to be thunder-makers!

hat! Da setz' einmal einer Seinesgleichen auf die moralische Art in die Welt! Man hat auch sein Fleisch und Blut! Ja, wenn ich ein Herr wär, und hätt' einen Hut und eine Uhr und ein Augenglas und könnt' vornehm reden, ich wollte schon tugendhaft sein! Es muss ein Schönes sein um die Tugend, Herr Hauptmann. Aber ich bin ein armer Kerl![1] Unsereins ist doch einmal unselig in dieser und der andern Welt! Ich glaub', wenn wir in den Himmel kämen, so müssten wir donnern helfen!

CAPTAIN

[Wozzeck! You've no sense of virtue! You're not a man of virtue! Flesh and blood? Whenever I lie by the window, when it's been raining, and watch the white stockings skipping down the street — dammit, Wozzeck, then I feel I'm in love! I'm flesh and blood, too! But Wozzeck, virtue! virtue! Then how would I spend the time? — I keep on telling myself that I'm a man of virtue,

[Wozzeck! Er hat keine Tugend, Er ist kein tugendhafter Mensch! Fleisch und Blut? Wenn ich am Fenster lieg', wenn's geregnet hat, und den weissen Strümpfen so nachseh', wie sie über die Gasse springen — verdammt! Wozzeck, da kommt mir die Liebe! Ich hab' auch Fleisch und Blut! Aber Wozzeck, die Tugend! die Tugend! Wie sollte ich dann die Zeit herumbringen? — ich sag' mir immer: du bist ein tugendhafter Mensch,

emotionally

a good person, a good person

ein guter Mensch, ein guter Mensch!

WOZZECK

[Yes, Sir, virtue — but that's not the way it works out for me. Look, common people like us don't have any virtue; we just do what comes naturally]

[Ja, Herr Hauptmann, die Tugend — ich hab's noch nicht so aus. Sehn Sie, wir gemeine Leut' — das hat keine Tugend; es kommt einem nur so die Natur.][2].

CAPTAIN
somewhat nonplussed

All right, all right! I know:

Schon gut, schon gut! Ich weiss:[3]

pacifying

that you're a worthy man,

Er ist ein guter Mensch,

exaggerating

a worthy man.

ein guter Mensch.

more controlled

But you think too much, that hurts; you always look so harassed.

Aber Er denkt zu viel, das zehrt; Er sieht immer so verhetzt aus.

anxiously

This discussion has quite unnerved me. Get along, but not at a run! Go quite slowly [, nice and slowly,] down the street on your way back, and keep to the middle . . .

Der Diskurs hat mich angegriffen. Geh' Er jetzt, und renn Er nicht so! Geh' Er langsam [, hübsch langsam] die Strasse hinunter, genau in der Mitte . . .

Wozzeck is about to leave in haste.

and once more, go quite slowly, quite slowly!

und nochmals, geh' Er langsam, hübsch langsam![4]

Exit Wozzeck. The curtain falls.

---

1. These three sentences ('wenn ich ein Herr wär . . . ein armer Kerl!') close Wozzeck's next speech after 'so die Natur' in the play. Berg omitted the Captain's speech and compressed the sequence. 2. See note above. 3. Berg simply had 'Gut, Wozzeck,' for this whole line. 4. Berg interpolated this final line.

Change of scene. [1]

Scene Two. *Open fields. The town in the distance. Late afternoon. Wozzeck and Andres are cutting sticks in the bushes.* [3]

WOZZECK
spoken

Hey, this place is accursed!	Du, der Platz ist verflucht!

ANDRES
working on, speaking

Go on!	Ach was!

singing to himself

The huntsman's life is one for me,	Das ist die schöne Jägerei,
shooting for all is free!	Schiessen steht Jedem frei!
I would a huntsman be.	Da möcht ich Jäger sein.
There would I be!	Da möcht ich hin!

WOZZECK

This place is accursed!	Der Platz ist verflucht!
See that bright streak of light above the grass there, where the toadstools are springing up? There rolls at dusk . . .	Siehst Du den lichten Streif da über das Gras hin, wo die Schwämme so nachwachsen? Da rollt Abends . . .

whispered

. . . a head.	. . . ein Kopf.

eventually singing

Once a man did lift it up, thought it was a hedgehog.	Hob ihn einmal Einer auf, meint' es wär' ein Igel.

singing

Three days and three nights later, he was laid in a wooden coffin.	Drei Tage und drei Nächte drauf, und er lag auf den Hobelspänen.

ANDRES
speaking

It gets darker. You are afraid. Go on!	Es wird finster, das macht Dir angst. Ei was!

Andres stops working, strikes a stance and starts singing. Wozzeck works on.

Over there a hare runs free,	Läuft dort ein Has' vorbei,
asks me if I huntsman be.	Fragt mich, ob ich Jäger sei?
Huntsman have I often been.	Jäger bin ich auch schon gewesen,
Try to shoot it . . .	Schiessen kann ich . . .

Wozzeck stops working.

. . . I cannot!	. . . aber nit!

WOZZECK
spoken

Quiet, Andres! That must be the Freemasons!	Still, Andres! Das waren die Freimaurer!

ANDRES

Two fat hares were sitting, eating off the greeny grass.	Sassen dort zwei Hasen, Frassen ab das grüne Gras.

He stops.

WOZZECK

That's it! The Freemasons! Quiet! Still!	Ich hab's! Die Freimaurer! Still! Still!

Both listen anxiously.

ANDRES
rather uneasy, in order to calm Wozzeck and himself, speaking

Sing it with me!	Sing lieber mit!

64

*Bodo Schwanbeck (Wozzeck) and Richard van Vrooman (Andres), Zurich, 1968; producer,
Lotfi Mansouri, designer, Max Röthlisberger (photo: Hertha Ramme)*

exuberantly

[Two hares were sitting there,]	[Sassen dort zwei Hasen,]
Eating off the greeny [greeny] grass.	Frassen ab das grüne [grüne] Gras.

Wozzeck stamps on the ground.

Down —	Bis —

He stops.

WOZZECK

[Do you hear, Andres; there's something	[Hörst du, Andres, es geht was?!] Hohl!
moving?] Hollow! All quite hollow!	Alles hohl!

ANDRES

— to the roots.	— auf den Ra(sen).

WOZZECK

A gulf! It quakes . . .	Ein Schlund! Es schwankt . . .

He staggers.

Listen, there's something moving with	Hörst Du, es wandert was mit uns da
us down there!	unten!

In mounting fear, he shouts.

Away!	Fort, fort!

He tries to pull Andres away.

ANDRES
holding Wozzeck back, speaking

Hey! Are you mad?	He, bist Du toll?

He stands still.

WOZZECK

It's strangely still and close. So close	's ist kurios still. Und schwül. Man
that your breathing seems to stop . . .	möchte den Atem anhalten . . .
[Andres!]	[Andres!]

He stares into the distance. The sun is just setting. The last rays make the horizon appear flooded with sunlight.

ANDRES
almost spoken

What?	Was?

WOZZECK

[Say something! Andres! How bright!]	[Red' was! Andres! wie hell!] Ein Feuer!
A fire! A fire! It rises from earth to	Ein Feuer! Das fährt von der Erde in
heaven and with a deafening clamour,	den Himmel und ein Getös' herunter,

Rather suddenly, twilight sets in, to which the eye only gradually becomes accustomed.

just like trumpets.	wie Posaunen.

shouting

It gets closer!	Wie's heranklirrt!

ANDRES
feigning calmness

The sun has set, hear the drummers.	Die Sonn' ist unter, drinnen trommeln
	sie.

He puts his sticks together.

WOZZECK

Still, [again] all is still, as if all the	Still, [wieder] Alles still, als wäre die
world's dead.	Welt tot.

ANDRES

Night! We must go home!	Nacht! Wir müssen heim!

Exeunt both slowly. Slow curtain.

Change of Scene. *Off-stage band music before the curtain rises.*

Scene Three. *Marie's room. Evening. Marie stands with her child on her arm, at the window. The band approaches. (The scene is spoken unless otherwise noted.)*

MARIE

Tschin, Bum, Tschin, Bum, Bum, Bum,   Tschin, Bum, Tschin, Bum, Bum, Bum,
Bum!   Bum!

The band approaches.

Do you hear, boy? They're coming now!   Hörst Bub? Da kommen sie!

The band, headed by the Drum Major, comes into the street before Marie's window.

MARGRET
peering into the window and saying to Marie

What a man! Like a tree!   Was ein Mann! Wie ein Baum!

MARIE
through the window, to Margret

Proud as a lion!   Er steht auf seinen Füssen wie ein Löw.

The Drum Major greets Marie, who waves to him.

MARGRET

Oho! What friendly eyes you're making!   Ei was freundliche Augen, Frau
We're not used to that from you! . . .   Nachbarin! So was is man an ihr nit
    gewohnt! . . .

MARIE
singing to herself

The soldiers, the soldiers are   [4]   Soldaten, Soldaten sind schöne
handsome fellows!   Burschen!

MARGRET
shouting through the window

Your eyes are [still] sparkling!   Ihre Augen glänzen ja [noch]!

MARIE
She stops singing.

So what? What's that to do with you?   Und wenn! Was geht Sie's an? Trag' Sie
Take your eyes to the jeweller and have   ihre Augen zum Juden, und lass Sie sie
them polished, so you can sell them for   putzen: Vielleicht glänzen sie auch noch,
two buttons.   dass man sie für zwei Knöpf verkaufen
    könnt'.

MARGRET

How dare you, 'Madam Virtuous'! I'm   Was Sie, Sie 'Frau Jungfer'! Ich bin eine
an honest woman, but everyone knows   honette Person, aber, Sie, das weiss
you can see your way through seven   Jeder, Sie guckt sieben Paar lederne
pairs of leather trousers!   Hosen durch!

MARIE
shouting at her

Bitch!   Luder!

She slams the window. The band music can no longer be heard. She is alone with the child. (From here on the scene is sung.)

Come, my boy! We won't hear their [5]   Komm, mein Bub! Was die Leute wollen!
slanders!

She takes the child in her arms, and sits down.

You're just a poor harlot's child, but   Bist nur ein arm Hurenkind und machst
give to your mother such real joy, although   Deiner Mutter doch so viel Freud' mit
no priest blessed your little face!   deinem unehrlichen Gesicht!

She rocks the child.

Hush a-bye baby . . .	Eia popeia . . .
Maiden, what song shall you sing? [6]	Mädel, was fangst Du jetzt an?
You have a child, but no ring!	Hast ein klein Kind und kein Mann!
Why such sorrow pursue,	Ei, was frag' ich darnach,
singing the whole night through:	Sing' ich die ganze Nacht:
Hush a-bye baby, my darling boy,	Eia popeia, mein süsser Bu'[1],
nobody cares, no not one!	Gibt mir kein Mensch nix dazu!
Johnny, go saddle your horses now,	Hansel, spann Deine sechs Schimmel an,
give them to eat and to spare —	Gib sie zu fressen auf's neu —
not oats to eat today,	Kein Haber fresse sie,
not water to drink today,	Kein Wasser saufe sie,
coolest, purest wine shall it be!	Lauter kühle Wein muss es sein!
[Hurrah!]	[Juchhe!]

She notices the child is asleep.

Coolest, purest wine shall it be!	Lauter kühle Wein muss es sein!

Marie is sunk in thought. [7] *There is a knock at the window. She starts with fright.*

Who's there?	Wer da?

She jumps up.

Is it you, Franz?	Bist Du's, Franz?

She opens the window.

Come to me!	Komm herein!

WOZZECK
through the window

No, no! Must go and report!	Kann nit! Muss in die Kasern'![2]

MARIE

Were you cutting canes in the field for the Captain?	Hast Stecken geschnitten für den Major?

WOZZECK

Yes, Marie. Ah . . .	Ja, Marie. Ach . . .

MARIE

What is it, Franz? You look so disturbed?	Was hast Du, Franz? Du siehst so verstört?

WOZZECK

Pst, hush! I found it out! A shape lay across the sky, and all was aglow! Yes, I think I understand!	Pst, Still! Ich hab's heraus! Es war ein Gebild am Himmel, und Alles in Glut! Ich bin Vielem auf der Spur!

MARIE

Franz!	Mann!

WOZZECK

But now all is darkness, darkness . . . Marie, there was something there,	Und jetzt Alles finster, finster . . . Marie, es war wieder was,

He reflects.

maybe . . .	vielleicht . . .

mysteriously

Is it not written: 'Behold, the smoke did rise from the Land, as if from a furnace.'	Steht nicht geschrieben: 'Und sieh, es ging der Rauch auf vom Land, wie ein Rauch vom Ofen.'

MARIE

Franz!	Franz!

---

1. mein Bub, juchhu! (rhyming with 'dazu') 2. zum Verles! to roll call!

And <u>it followed me all the way</u> back into the town.

Es ist hinter mir hergegangen bis vor die Stadt.

in great excitement

<u>Now what will happen?</u>

Was soll das werden?

MARIE
Perplexed, she tries to calm him and shows him the child.

Franz! Franz! <u>Your child!</u>

Franz! Franz! Dein Bub!

WOZZECK
absently

<u>My child</u> . . .

Mein Bub . . .

without looking at him, still absently

My child . . . [Hey! Little man! D'you want to go to the fair this evening? I've saved some money.] I must be off.

Mein Bub . . . [Hei, Jung! Heut abend wieder auf die Mess! Ich hab' noch was gespart!] Jetzt muss ich fort.

He rushes off. Marie leaves the window.

MARIE
alone with the child, looking at him anxiously [7]

That man! So distracted! He did not even look at his child! He will crack up with all that thinking! You are so still, boy. Frightened? It's now as dark here as if one were blind: even the street lamp is not lit tonight!

Der Mann! So vergeistert! Er hat sein Kind nicht angesehn! Er schnappt noch über mit den Gedanken! Was bist so still, Bub. Fürch'st Dich? Es wird so dunkel, man meint, man wird blind; sonst scheint doch die Latern' herein!

She breaks out in sudden anguish.

Ah! <u>Poor folk like us.</u> I can't go on . . . I'm trembling . . . [5]

Ach! Wir arme Leut. Ich halt's nit aus . . . Es schauert mich . . . ←

She rushes to the door. The curtain falls quickly.

Change of scene [5] *The curtain rises quickly.*

Scene Four. *The Doctor's study. A sunny afternoon. Wozzeck enters. The Doctor rushes to meet Wozzeck as he comes in the door.*

DOCTOR

<u>You've disgraced me,</u> Wozzeck! <u>Where is your word?</u> Eh, Eh, Eh!

Was erleb' ich, Wozzeck? Ein Mann ein[1] Wort? Ei, ei, ei!

WOZZECK

What, Sir? What, Doctor?

Was denn, Herr Doktor?

DOCTOR

I saw you now, Wozzeck, I saw you just <u>now coughing in the street.</u> You were coughing, you howled like a dog.[3] You do not get paid every day for such antics! Wozzeck! This is bad! <u>The world is bad,</u> so bad! Oh!

Ich habs gesehn, Wozzeck, Er hat wieder gehustet, auf der Strasse gehustet,[2] ⊀ gebellt wie ein Hund! Geb' ich Ihm dafür alle Tage drei Groschen? Wozzeck! Das ist schlecht! Die Welt ist[4] schlecht, sehr schlecht! Oh!

WOZZECK
groaning

Listen please, Doctor, when <u>forced to it by Nature!</u>

Aber Herr Doktor, wenn Einem die Natur kommt!

---

1. von Wort — of your word 2. gep—t, auf die Strasse gep—t — <u>pissing</u>, pissing in the street 3. <s>Berg's alteration to 'gehustet'</s> — coughed — makes the Doctor's reaction even more ⊀ peculiar. A modern version of the libretto could restore Büchner's original: 'pissing in the street. You were pissing on the wall like a dog.' George Perle observes 'These revisions were not due to any personal squeamishness on Berg's part but to the simple fact that retention of Büchner's original text in this scene would have inevitably precluded performance of the work on any operatic stage of the time.' This would entail adjustments throughout the rest of the scene. 4. wird — getting

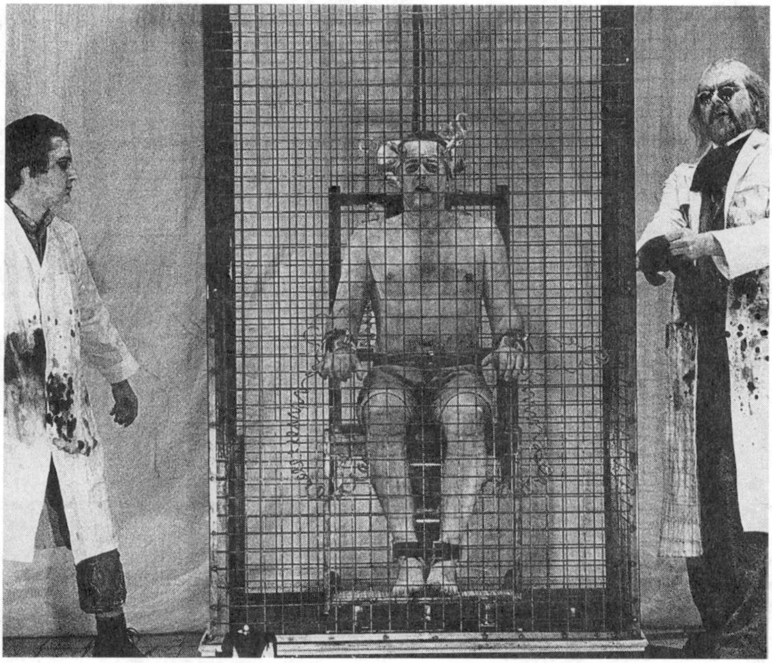

Above: Benjamin Luxon (Wozzeck) and Roderick Kennedy (Doctor), Scottish Opera, 1983; producer, David Alden, designer, David Fielding (photo: Eric Thorburn). Below: Donald McIntyre as the Doctor, Covent Garden, 1984 (photo: Clive Barda)

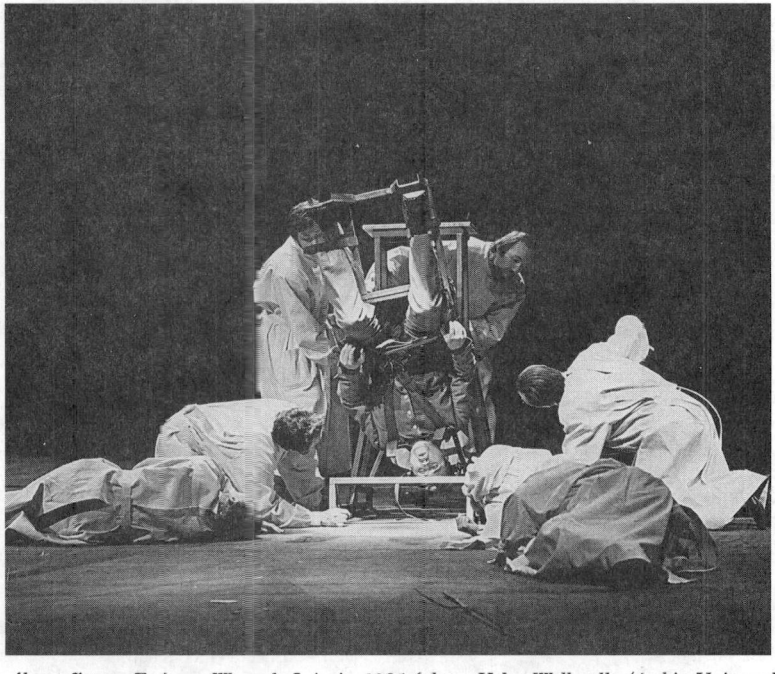

Above: Jürgen Freier as Wozzeck, Leipzig, 1985 (photo: Helga Wallmüller/Archiv Universal Edition). 'Wozzeck', Welsh National Opera, 1986, produced and designed by Liviu Ciulei (photo: Clive Barda)

By Nature! By Nature! Superstition,
ridiculous superstition! [Nature!] Have I
not demonstrated that the muscles are
subject to the human will? Nature's
force, Wozzeck! Man's will is free! In
man, individuality is sublimated into
freedom! [Can't hold your urine!]

shaking his head, to himself

(You were coughing!)

again to Wozzeck

Have you already eaten your beans up,
Wozzeck?

Wozzeck nods.

Only beans, nothing else but beans!
Mark my words! And in three months ✕
we'll start with a little leg of mutton.
I'm starting a whole revolution in
medicine: [I'm blowing the whole thing
sky-high. Urine, ammonium hyper-
chlorate, hyperoxide. Can't you have
another piss? Go outside and try again.

WOZZECK

[I can't, Doctor.

DOCTOR
angrily

[But pissing up against the wall! I've a
written undertaking, in your own hand.
I saw you, with my very own eyes — I'd
just stuck my nose out of the window
and was letting the sun play on it in
order to observe myself sneezing, to see
what starts a person sneezing. You must
observe everything. Have you caught
any frogs for me? Frogspawn? Freshwater
polyps? *Cristatellum?* Have you? Mind
the microscope, there's a ciliate's left
molar on the slide. But . . .

launching out at him

You pissed up against the wall! — No!
— I refuse to get angry, anger is
unhealthy, unscientific! I'm calm,
completely calm, my pulse is its usual
sixty, and I'm talking to you with
complete equanimity. God forbid I should
ever lose my temper over a human
being, a human being! If it had been a
proteus that had died on me! But,
Wozzeck, you shouldn't have pissed
against the wall!]

Die Natur kommt! Die Natur kommt!
Aberglaube, abscheulicher Aberglaube!
[Die Natur!] Hab' ich nicht nachgewiesen,
dass das Zwerchfell[1] dem Willen
unterworfen ist? Die Natur, Wozzeck!
Der Mensch ist frei! In dem Menschen
verklärt sich die Individualität zur Freiheit!
[Den Harn nicht halten können!]

(Husten müssen!)

Hat Er schon seine Bohnen[2] gegessen,
Wozzeck?

Nichts als Bohnen[2], nichts als
Hülsenfrüchte! Merk Er sich's! Die
nächste Woche fangen wir dann mit
Schöpsenfleisch[3] an. Es gibt eine
Revolution in der Wissenschaft: [ich
sprenge sie in die Luft. Harnstoff,
salzsaures Ammonium, Hyperoxydul! —
Wozzeck, kann Er nicht wieder p--n?
Geh' Er einmal da hinein und probir
Er's.

[Ich kann nit, Herr Docter!

[Aber an die Wand p—n! Ich hab's
schriftlich, den Accord in der Hand! Ich
hab's geseh'n, mit diesen Augen gesehen,
ich steckte gerade die Nase zum Fenster
hinaus und liess die Sonnenstrahlen
hineinfallen, um das Niesen zu
beobachten, die Entstehung des Niesens.
Man muss alles beobachten. Hat er mir
Frösche gefangen? Laich? Süsswasser-
Polypen? *Cristatellum?* Hat Er? Stoss' Er
mir nicht ans Mikroskop, ich habe
den linken Backenzahn eines Infusoriums
darunter. Aber . . .

Er hat an die Wand gep—t! —[4] Nein! —
ich ärgere mich nicht, ärgern ist
ungesund, ist unwissenschaftlich! Ich bin
ruhig, ganz ruhig, mein Puls hat seine
gewöhnlichen 60, und ich sag's Ihm mit
der grössten Kaltblütigkeit. Behüte, wer
wird sich über einen Menschen ärgern,
einen Menschen! Wenn es noch ein
Proteus wäre, der einem unpässlich
wird! Aber, Wozzeck, Er hätte doch
nicht an die Wand p—n sollen!]

---

1. ie. diaphragm: Büchner had 'der *musculus sphincter vesicae*' ie. bladder 2. Erbsen — peas
3. Hammelfleisch — mutton 4. The rest of this speech was incorporated in the libretto by
Berg into the Doctor's next paragraph (see overleaf).

counting on his fingers

Albumen, fats, carbohydrates:	Eiweiss, Fette, Kohlenhydrate;

making a broad gesture

and next: Oxyaldehydanhydridum ...	und zwar: Oxyaldehydanhydride ...

with another gesture, and then with sudden anger

And yet, you have once again failed me ...	Aber, Er hat wieder gehustet ...

He goes up to Wozzeck, then checks himself.

No! This anger will not do, anger is bad for health, and unscientific! I am quite calm, my pulse is beating its regular sixty, take care and do not let a mere man upset you! If it were some guinea pig which had lost all self-control ...	Nein! Ich ärgere mich nicht, ärgern ist ungesund, ist unwissenschaftlich! Ich bin ganz ruhig, mein Puls hat seine gewöhnlichen Sechzig, behüt, wer wird sich über einen Menschen ärgern! Wenn es noch ein Molch wäre, der einem unpässlich wird.

vigorously

But now, really, Wozzeck, you really need not misbehave so!	Aber, aber, Wozzeck, Er hätte doch nicht husten sollen!

WOZZECK

pacifying the Doctor, who is making furious gestures

But listen, Doctor, sometimes people have dispositions, they're made that way; and yet, and yet with Nature it's different.	Seh'n Sie, Herr Doktor, manchmal hat man so 'nen Charakter, so 'ne Struktur; aber mit der Natur ist's was ander's.

snapping his fingers [7]

See now, with Nature it is like [, like] ... how shall I describe it ... for example: when Nature has ...	Sehn Sie, mit der Natur, ... das ist so [was] ... wie soll ich denn sagen ... zum Beispiel: Wenn die Natur ...

DOCTOR

Wozzeck, again you're philosophising! What, when Nature has?	Wozzeck, Er philosophiert wieder! Was? Wenn die Natur? ...

WOZZECK

When Nature has vanished, and the world's so dark, so dark, that you have to grope round it with your hands searchingly, and it seems to disperse like a spider's web. Ah! When it's there and is not there! Ah, ah, Marie! When all around is dark,	Wenn die Natur aus ist, wenn die Welt so finster wird, dass man mit den Händen an ihr herum tappen muss, dass man weint, sie verrinnt, wie [ein] Spinnengewebe. Ach, wenn was ist und [5] doch nicht is! Ach, Ach, Marie! Wenn Alles dunkel is,

He takes a few steps across the room with outstretched arms.

and from out the west, red light is glowing, as from out a furnace oh, what, what is there to cling to?	und nur noch ein roter Schein im Westen, wie von einer Esse: an was soll man sich da halten?

DOCTOR

Man, you're feeling your way around with your feet as with spider's legs.	Kerl, Er tastet mit seinen Füssen herum, wie mit Spinnenfüssen.

WOZZECK

close to the Doctor, in a confidential tone

But, Doctor, [Have you ever seen anything of dual nature?] when at midday the sun is high and it seems the world is bursting forth in flame, just at that time terrifying voices are speaking to me.	Herr Doktor, [haben Sie schon was von der doppelten Natur gesehen?] Wenn die Sonne im Mittag steht, und es ist, als ging' die Welt in Feuer auf, hat schon eine fürchterliche Stimme zu mir geredet.

DOCTOR

Wozzeck, you have got an aberration.	Wozzeck, Er hat eine aberratio.

The toadstools! Haven't you seen the rings of the toadstools out there on the ground? Lines and circles, strange figures — [it's written there] — would that one could read them!

Die Schwämme! Haben Sie schon die Ringe von den Schwämmen am Boden gesehn? Linienkreise, Figuren — [da steckts, da] — Wer das lesen könnte!

DOCTOR

Wozzeck, your mind is wandering. You are quite obsessed by an *idée fixe*, such an excellent aberratio mentalis partialis, second species! Nicely cultivated! Wozzeck, you'll get an extra payment! [Second species: *idée fixe* in a generally rational state.] You carry on as before? You still shave the Captain? You'll catch my leeches? Eating your beans up?

[8] Wozzeck, Er kommt ins Narrenhaus. Er hat eine schöne fixe Idee, eine köstliche aberratio mentalis partialis, zweite Spezies! Sehr schön ausgebildet! Wozzeck, Er kriegt noch mehr Zulage! [Zweite Spezies: Fixe Idee bei allgemein vernünftigem Zustand!] Tut Er[1] noch Alles wie sonst? Rasiert seinen Hauptmann? Fängt fleissig Molche? Isst seine Bohnen[2]?

WOZZECK

I do everything you tell me. I need this money for my wife: that is why I do it![4]

Immer ordentlich, Herr Doktor, denn das Menagegeld[3] kriegt das Weib: Darum tu' ich's ja![4]

DOCTOR

You are a most absorbing case. Keep it up, my man! Wozzeck, I'll give you one more penny extra payment. But now what must you do?

Er ist ein interessanter Fall, halt' Er sich nur brav! Wozzeck, Er kriegt noch einen Groschen mehr Zulage. Was muss Er aber tun?

---

1. Er thut 2. Erbsen — peas 3. Das Geld für die Menage — money for the housekeeping
4. Büchner's scene continues as follows:

DOCTOR

Performing your duties?

Thut seinen Dienst?

WOZZECK

Yes, Sir.

Ja wohl!

DOCTOR

An interesting case! You'll get an extra ha'penny a week! Be a good boy, Wozzeck! Look at me: what do you have to do?

Er ist ein interessanter Casus! Er kriegt noch einen Groschen Zulage die Woche. Wozzeck, halt' Er sich nur brav! Seh' Er mich an: was muss Er thun?

WOZZECK
groaning

Marie . . .

Die Marie . . .

DOCTOR

Eat your peas, then eat some mutton, clean your rifle and in the meantime cultivate this *idée fixe* of yours. Oh, what a theory! I'll be famous! I'll be immortal! Immortal!

Erbsen essen, dann Hammelfleisch essen, sein Gewehr putzen, dazwischen die fixe Idee pflegen. O, meine Theorie! O, mein Ruhm! Ich werde unsterblich! Unsterblich!

WOZZECK

Yes, but Marie . . . and the poor brat.

Ja! die Marie . . . und der arme Wurm.

DOCTOR

Immortal, Wozzeck! Show me your tongue!

Unsterblich, Wozzeck! Zeig' er die Zunge!

74

not bothering about the Doctor

Ah, Marie!	[5] Ach, Marie!

DOCTOR

What must you do?	Was muss Er tun?

WOZZECK

Marie!	Marie!

DOCTOR

What?	Was?

WOZZECK

Ah!	Ach!

DOCTOR

Eat your beans up. For three months,	Bohnen essen, dann Schöpsenfleisch
just beans then, no coughing[1], go on	essen, nicht husten, seinen Hauptmann
shaving the Captain, and cultivate your	rasieren, dazwischen die fixe Idee
idée fixe further! Oh!	pflegen! Oh!

waxing ecstatic

My hypothesis! Oh, my fame! I shall be	Meine Theorie! Oh, mein Ruhm! Ich
immortal! Immortal! Immortal!	werde unsterblich! Unsterblich!
	Unsterblich!

at the height of ecstasy

Immortal!	Unsterblich!

suddenly quite calm, walking up to Wozzeck

Wozzeck, let me look at your tongue,	Wozzeck, zeig' Er mir jetzt die Zunge!
now!	

Wozzeck obeys.

The curtain falls at first quickly, then suddenly slowly and at last closes quite gradually.

Change of scene to Scene Five.

The next two scenes are not in the libretto.

Public place. Booths. *Townspeople, Wozzeck, Marie.*

OLD MAN AND CHILD
dancing and singing

Nothing lasts upon this earth,	Auf der Welt ist kein Bestand,
All of us must die as sure as we are	Wir müssen alle sterben, das ist uns
given birth.	wohlbekannt.
So raise a cheer! And on we go!	Heissassa! Hopssassa!

WOZZECK

Hey, Marie, cheer up! It's a beautiful	He! Marie, lustig! Schöne Welt! Gelt?
world, surely?	

SHOWMAN
outside his tent

Ladies and gentlemen! Come and see	Meine Herren und Damen! Hier sind zu
the Astronomical Horse and the	sehen das astronomische Pferd und der
Geographical Donkey! As made by God,	geographische Esel! Die Kreatur, wie sie
creatures are nothing, nothing at all! But	Gott gemacht hat, ist nix, gar nix! Sehen
look what art can do! Even the monkey	Sie die Kunst! Schon der Affe hier! Geht
here! Walking upright, wearing a coat	aufrecht, hat Rock und Hosen, hat einen
and trousers and carrying a sword! Hey,	Säbel! He, Michel! mach Kompliment!
Mick! Bow to the ladies and gentlemen!	So ist's brav! Gib' Kuss. Da!
Well done! Give us a kiss! There!	

---

1. Again, Berg's version has 'coughing' for 'pissing', which a modern version might replace.

The monkey makes a trumpeting sound.

Ladies and Gentlemen! Come and see the Historical Horse and the Philosophical Donkey. They're favourites of all the crowned heads of Europe, Africa and Australia. Members of all the learned societies, formerly professors at one of our ancient universities. The donkey tells people everything, how old they are, how many children they've got, what their illnesses are! I'm not having you on, it's all strictly educational! The donkey has beastly powers of reason or rather it's reasonably beastly: it's not as stupid as a beast, as humans are, present company excepted. The monkey can walk upright and fire a pistol, he's musical.

Meine Herren und Damen! Hier sind zu sehen das historische Pferd und der philosophische Esel. Sind Favorits von allen Potentaten Europas, Afrikas, Australiens. Mitglieder von allen gelehrten Gesellschaften, waren früher Professoren an einer Universität. Der Esel sagt den Leuten alles, wie alt, wie viel Kinder, was für Krankheiten! Kein Schwindel, alles Erziehung! Der Esel hat eine viehische Vernunft, auch vernünftige Viehigkeit, ist nicht viehdumm, wie die Menschen, das geehrte Publikum abgerechnet. Der Aff' geht aufrecht, schiesst eine Pistolelos, ist musikalisch.

The monkey makes another trumpeting noise.

Ladies and gentlemen! Come and see the Astronomical Donkey, the Romantic Horse, the Military Ape! Roll up, roll up, the beginning's about to begin. Walk right in, it'll only cost you a ha'penny.

Meine Herren und Damen! Hier sind zu sehen der astrologische Esel, das romantische Pferd, der militärische Affe! Hereinspaziert, meine Herrschaften, gleich ist der Anfang vom Anfang. Hereinspaziert, kost einen Groschen!

FIRST ONLOOKER

I'm a great lover of the grotesque. I'm an atheist.

Ich bin ein Freund vom Grotesken. Ich bin ein Atheist.

SECOND ONLOOKER

I'm a dogmatic Christian atheist. I must see the donkey.

Ich bin ein christlich-dogmatischer Atheist. Ich muss den Esel sehen.

They enter the tent.

WOZZECK

You want to go in?

Willst auch hinein?

MARIE

I don't mind. Just look at the man's tassels! And the woman's wearing trousers! It must be quite something!

Mein'twegen. Was der Mensch Quasten hat, und die Frau hat Hosen. Das muss ein schön Ding sein.

They go inside.

Inside one of the booths.

SHOWMAN
producing the donkey

Show your paces now! Show them your beastly reason. Put human society to shame. Ladies and gentlemen, this donkey that you see before you with four hooves and a tail and all the usual accessories was a professor at one of our universities, where he taught the students how to ride and fight! He has a simple understanding but dual powers of reason. What do you do when you think with dual reason?

Zeig dein Talent! zeig deine viehische Vernünftigkeit. Beschäme die menschliche *Société*. Meine Herrschaften, das ist ein Esel, hat vier Hufe und einen Schweif und das sonstige Zubehör! War Professor an einer Universität, die Studenten haben bei ihm Reiten und Schlagen gelernt! Er hat einen einfachen Verstand und eine doppelte Raison. Was machst du, wenn du mit der doppelten Raison denkst?

The donkey pisses.

When you think with dual reason?! Tell me, is there a donkey among our distinguished audience?

Wenn du mit der doppelten Raison denkst?! Sage, ist unter der geehrten *Société* da ein Esel?

The donkey shakes its head.

You see, that's reason for you. What's the difference between a human being and a donkey? They're both dust, sand and filth. Only the way they express themselves is different. The donkey talks with its hoof. Tell the ladies and gentlemen what time it is? Does anyone here have a watch?

Sehen Sie, das ist Vernunft. Was ist der Unterschied zwischen einem Menschen und einem Esel? Staub, Sand, Dreck sind beide. Nur das Ausdrücken ist verschieden. Der Esel spricht mit dem Huf. Sag' den Herrschaften, wie viel Uhr es ist! Wer von den Herrschaften hat eine Uhr?

A MEMBER OF THE CROWD
handing him his watch

Here!

Hier!

MARIE

I must see this.

Das muss ich sehen!

She climbs on to a bench.

WOZZECK

— — —

Scene Five. *Street before the door of Marie's dwelling. Evening twilight.* [9]

MARIE
standing in admiration in front of the Drum Major

Let's see you march again!

Geh' einmal vor Dich hin!

The Drum Major pulls himself up straight, and marches a few steps.

He has a chest like a bull and a beard like a lion. No one like him! I'm the proudest woman in the world!

[4] Über die Brust wie ein Stier[1] und ein Bart wie ein Löwe. So ist Keiner! Ich
[10] bin stolz vor allen Weibern!

DRUM MAJOR
[9]

Wait till on a Sunday I wear my plumes in my cap, and my fine white gloves, too! Saints almighty! The Prince himself says: 'Now there is a real man.'

Wenn ich erst am Sonntag den grossen
[10] Federbusch hab', und die weissen Handschuh! Donnerwetter! Der Prinz sagt immer: Mensch! Er ist ein Kerl!

MARIE
mockingly

So what?

Ach was!

She walks up to him admiringly.

Man!

Mann!

DRUM MAJOR

And you're a ripe young woman! Snakes alive! We'll start a proper stud of future Drum Majors right now. Well?

Und Du, bist auch ein Weibsbild! Sapperment! Wir wollen eine Zucht von Tambourmajors anlegen. Was?![2]

He embraces her.

MARIE

Let go!

Lass mich!

She tries to break loose. They wrestle. [9]

DRUM MAJOR

Savage beast!

Wildes Tier!

---

1. ein Rind — a bull 2. He!

77

Anja Silja (Marie) and James King (Drum Major), Covent Garden, 1984; producer, Willy Decker, designer, Caspar Neher (photo: Clive Barda)

MARIE
breaking free

Keep your hands off!	Rühr mich nicht an!

DRUM MAJOR
He draws himself up to his full height, and steps close to Marie, ingratiatingly.

Is it the devil in your eyes?	Sieht Dir der Teufel aus den Augen?!

He embraces her again, with almost menacing determination.

MARIE

What's it matter? It is all the same!	Meinetwegen, es ist Alles eins!

[9]

She falls into his arms, and disappears with him through the open door. [1]

Slow curtain. End of Act One.

The next scene is not in the opera.

The Doctor's Courtyard. *Students and Wozzeck (below), the Doctor (at the attic window).*

DOCTOR

Gentlemen! Here I am, standing on the roof like David when he saw Bathsheba; but all I can see are some *culs de Paris* hanging out to dry in the gardens of the girls' boarding school. Gentlemen! We are here to discuss the important question of the relation of subject to object. If we take one of those creatures in which the organic self-affirmation of the divine is most clearly manifest from so high a standpoint and if we examine its relation to space, the earth and time, gentlemen, if I take this cat and throw it out of the window, how will it react vis-à-vis the law of gravity and its own natural instinct? Hey, Wozzeck!	Meine Herren! Ich bin auf dem Dache wie David, als er die Bathseba sah; aber ich sehe nichts, als die *culs de Paris* der Mädchenpension im Garten trocknen. Meine Herren! Wir sind an der wichtigen Frage über das Verhältniss des Subjekts zum Objekt. Wenn wir eins von den Dingen nehmen, worin sich die organische Selbst-Affirmation des Göttlichen auf einem so hohen Standpunkte manifestirt, und ihr Verhältniss zum Raum, zur Erde, zur Zeit untersuchen, meine Herren, wenn ich also diese Katze zum Fenster hinauswerfe, wie wird diese Wesenheit sich zum Gesetz der Gravitation und zum eigenen Instinkt verhalten? He, Wozzeck!

bellowing

Wozzeck!	Wozzeck!

WOZZECK
catching the cat

Doctor, it bites!	Herr Doctor, sie beisst!

DOCTOR

God dammit, you caught the beast so tenderly, it's as though it was your own grandmother.	Kerl! Er greift die Bestie so zärtlich an, als wär's seine Grossmutter.

WOZZECK

Doctor, I can't stop shaking.	Herr Doctor, ich hab' Zittern.

DOCTOR
delighted

Haha! Wonderful, Wozzeck.	Haha! schön, Wozzeck.

He rubs his hands.

WOZZECK

I feel faint.	Mir wird dunkel!

79

DOCTOR

descending to the courtyard and taking the cat

What's this I see, gentlemen? A new species of hare louse. A more beautiful species than any that's already known.

Was seh' ich, meine Herren? Eine neue Species Hasenlaus. Eine schönere Species als die bekannte.

He takes out a magnifying glass.

A hare louse, gentlemen!

Hasenlaus, meine Herren!

The cat decamps.

Gentlemen, the animal has no scientific instinct. A hare louse, the finest examples of which are to be found in cats' fur. — Gentlemen! Let me show you something else instead. Look at this man here! For three months he's eaten nothing but peas! Note the effect — feel how irregular his pulse is, and then there are his eyes —

Meine Herren! Das Thier hat keinen wissenschaftlichen Instinkt. Hasenlaus, die schönsten Exemplare trägt es im Pelzwerk. — Meine Herren! Sie können dafür was anderes sehen. Sehen Sie diesen Menschen! Seit einem Vierteljahr isst er nichts als Erbsen! Bemerken Sie die Wirkung — fühlen einmal den ungleichen Puls, und dann die Augen —

WOZZECK

Doctor, I feel quite faint!

Herr Doctor, mir wird ganz dunkel!

He sits down.

DOCTOR

Cheer up, Wozzeck, only a few more days and then it'll all be over. Feel him, gentlemen, feel him!

Courage, Wozzeck, noch ein paar Tage, und dann ist's fertig. Fühlen Sie, meine Herren, fühlen Sie!

The students feel Wozzeck's temples, pulse and chest.

That reminds me, Wozzeck, why don't you wiggle your ears for these gentlemen. I meant to show you this before — two muscles are involved here. Come on! Get on with it!

A propos, Wozzeck, beweg' er vor den Herren doch einmal die Ohren. Ich hab's Ihnen schon zeigen wollen — zwei Muskeln sind dabei tätig. Allons! frisch!

WOZZECK

But, Doctor!

Ach, Herr Doctor!

DOCTOR

Do I have to wiggle them for you, you animal! Are you going to be like that cat? There, gentlemen! What you see here is, as it were, a transitional stage between man and donkey, frequently the result of female upbringing and the mother tongue. Wozzeck! It looks as though your mother pulled out most of your hair when she said goodbye to you, no doubt out of tenderness. You've gone very thin on top. Or is it only during the last few days? Is it the peas? Yes, gentlemen, the peas, it's the peas. There's science for you!

Bestie! Soll ich dir die Ohren bewegen! Willst du's machen, wie die Katze? So, meine Herren, das sind so Uebergänge zum Esel, häufig auch infolge weiblicher Erziehung und der Muttersprache. Wozzeck! Deine Haare hat die Mutter zum Abschied schön ausgerissen aus Zärtlichkeit. Sie sind ja ganz dünn geworden. Oder ist's erst seit ein paar Tagen, machen's die Erbsen? Ja, meine Herren, die Erbsen, die Erbsen! Die Wissenschaft!

Act Two

Scene One. *Marie's room. Morning, sunshine. Marie, with her child on her lap, is looking at herself in a piece of broken mirror.*

MARIE

(ear-rings)

How the stones do glisten! I wonder what they are? What was it he said?	Was die Steine glänzen? Was sind's für welche? Was hat er gesagt?

She thinks awhile. Then, turning to her child who has stirred

Sleep, child! Press your eyelids shut, tightly!	Schlaf, Bub! Drück die Augen zu, fest!

The child hides his eyes behind his hands.

Tighter! Like that!	Noch fester! Bleib so!

The child moves again.

Still, or else the bogeyman!	Still, oder er holt Dich!

with a feigned eeriness of expression, but roguish, almost wanton

Hush now, shut lattice tight. [6] Here comes a gipsy spright, who'll take you by the hand — out to gipsyland.	Mädel, mach's Lädel zu! 's kommt ein Zigeunerbu', Führt Dich an seiner Hand — Fort ins Zigeunerland.

The child, very frightened, has hidden his head in the folds of his mother's dress and keeps quite still. Marie looks at herself in the mirror.

Surely they're gold! Folk like us have but a corner in the world and a piece of mirror.	's ist gewiss Gold! Unsereins hat nur ein Eckchen in der Welt und ein Stückchen Spiegel.

with intensity

And yet — I have surely as red a mouth as the noble rich ladies who have their mirrors from ceiling to floor, and all their handsome lords, who take up their hands and kiss them; but I am just a poor wretched woman!	Und doch — hab' ich einen so roten Mund, als die grossen Madamen mit ihren Spiegeln von oben bis unten und ihren schönen Herrn, die ihnen die [5] Hände küssen; aber ich bin nur ein armes Weibsbild!

The child sits up.

crossly

Quiet! Boy! And close your eyes!	Still! Bub! Die Augen zu!

She flickers the mirror.

The sandman is here; he's on the wall there . . .	Das Schlafengelchen; wie's an der Wand läuft . . .

The child does not obey.

almost angry

Shut your eyes up tight! [6]	Mach die Augen zu!

Marie flickers the mirror again.

If he looks into your eyes, you'll be blinded, child.	Oder es sieht Dir hinein, dass Du blind wirst . . .

Wozzeck enters behind Marie. She does not notice him at first. She remains motionless with the intimidated child, waiting to see the effect of her game with the mirror. Then she suddenly jumps up and puts her hands to her ears.

WOZZECK

What's that there?	Was hast da?

MARIE

Nothing!	Nix!

WOZZECK

Something's shining through your fingers.	Unter Deinen Fingern glänzt's ja.

81

MARIE

A small earring, I just found it.   Ein Ohr-Ringlein, hab's gefunden.

He looks at the earring questioningly.

WOZZECK

I have never found things of that sort,   Ich hab so was nicht gefunden,
somewhat menacingly
two together.   zwei auf einmal.

MARIE
flaring up

D'you think I'm a whore?   Bin ich ein schlecht Mensch?

WOZZECK
calming her

Alright, Marie. Alright.   's ist gut, Marie! 's ist gut.
turning to the child
He's so deeply asleep! Take his arm and   Was der Bub immer schläft! Greif ihm
lift him, he's lying on it and beads of   unter's Ärmchen, der Stuhl drückt ihn.
sweat are forming on his brow . . . All   Die hellen Tropfen stehn ihm auf der
our days spent endlessly working, even   Stirn . . . Nichts als Arbeit unter der
sweat in sleep. Poor folk like us!   [2] Sonne, sogar Schweiss im Schlaf. Wir
   arme Leut!
in quite a different voice
Here is some more money, Marie,   Da ist wieder Geld, Marie,
counting it out into her hand
my wages, this from the Captain,   die Löhnung und was vom[1] Hauptmann
and the Doctor.   und vom Doktor.

MARIE

Bless you, Franz.   Gott vergelts, Franz.

WOZZECK

I must go, [this evening,] Marie . . .   Ich muss fort, [Heut Abend,] Marie . . .
Goodbye!   Adies!

Exit.

MARIE
alone

I am just a whore! I could kill myself for   Ich bin doch ein schlecht Mensch. Ich
it. Oh! This world! It all goes to the   könnt mich erstechen. Ach! Was Welt!
devil: man and wife and child!   Geht doch Alles zum Teufel: Mann und
   Weib und Kind![2]

Quick curtain.

Change of scene.

[6]

Scene Two. *Street in the town. Day. The Captain and Doctor meet each other.* [1]

CAPTAIN
coming onto the stage

You go too quickly, respected friend, Mr   Wohin so eilig, geehrtester Herr
Grave-digger.   Sargnagel?

DOCTOR
in a great hurry

You go too slowly, respected friend, old   Wohin so langsam, geehrtester Herr
Mr Square-basher.   Exercizengel?

He hurries on.

---

1. meinem Hauptmann — my Captain 2. und Kind! — added by Berg.

82

Why not take your time! | Nehmen Sie sich Zeit!

He tries to catch up.

DOCTOR

I can't! | Pressiert!

CAPTAIN
with the Doctor, who hastens on

Don't run so fast, man! Uff! | Laufen Sie nicht so! Uff!
taking a deep, noisy breath
Don't run so fast! A worthy man should | Laufen Sie nicht! Ein guter Mensch geht
not run so fast. | nicht so schnell.
His voice cracks.
A worthy man . . . | Ein guter Mensch . . .

DOCTOR

I have no time! | Pressiert, pressiert!

CAPTAIN
more and more breathless

A worthy . . You're chasing yourself | Ein guter . . . Sie hetzen sich ja hinter
into the grave-yard! [You're making me | dem Tod d'rein! [Sie machen mir Angst!
worried! |

DOCTOR

[I'm not wasting my time. | [Ich stehle meine Zeit nicht.

CAPTAIN

[A good person — | [Ein guter Mensch —
seizing the Doctor by the coat
[Doctor, horses terrify me when I think | [Herr Doctor, die Pferde machen mir
that the poor beasts have to go | ganz Angst, wenn ich denke, dass die
everywhere on foot. Don't run like that, | armen Bestien zu Fuss gehen müssen.
you old coffin-filler! And stop waving | Rennen Sie nicht so, Herr Sargnagel!
your stick in the air. You'll wear your | Rudern Sie mit dem Stock nicht so in
legs down to the pavement!] | der Luft! Sie schleifen sich ja Ihre Beine
 | auf dem Pflaster ab.]

*The Doctor slows down a little so that the Captain catches him up and plucks several times at
his coat.*

DOCTOR
irritably

I can't get the time to spare now. | Ich kann meine Zeit nicht stehlen.

CAPTAIN

A worthy man . . . | Ein guter Mensch . . .

DOCTOR

I can't, I have no time! | Pressiert, pressiert, pressiert!

CAPTAIN

But please don't run so fast, Doctor | Aber rennen Sie nicht so. Herr
Grave-digger! You're wearing your feet | Sargnagel! Sie schleifen ja Ihre Beine
and legs out on these paving stones. | auf dem Pflaster ab. Erlauben Sie,
Allow me, Sir,
The Captain is panting between words and the Doctor has stopped at last.
to save a fellow human . . | dass ich ein Menschenleben . . .
slowly calming down
being . . . | rette . . .

*The Doctor moves off slowly. The Captain takes another breath. The Doctor decides to listen to the
Captain.*

83

DOCTOR

Her! Within four weeks, dead!	Frau, in vier Wochen tot!

standing still

Cancer uteri.	Cancer uteri.

The Captain is getting uneasy.

I have had twenty similar patients to her —	Habe schon zwanzig solche Patienten gehabt —

about to move on

Within four weeks —	In vier Wochen —

CAPTAIN

Doctor, don't frighten me like that! There are some people who've died of shock, of pure and simple shock!	Doktor, erschrecken Sie mich nicht! Es [1] sind schon Leute am Schreck gestorben, am puren hellen Schreck!

DOCTOR

Within four weeks! She will make an interesting corpse.	In vier Wochen! Gibt ein intressantes Präparat.

He stands quite still and observes the Captain cold-bloodedly.

CAPTAIN

Oh, oh, oh . . .	Oh, oh, oh . . .

DOCTOR
in a pleasant tone

As for you! Hmm! Bloated features, fat, thickish neck, apoplectical constitution there! Yes, dear Captain,	Und Sie selbst! Hm! Aufgedunsen, fett, dicker Hals, apoplektische Konstitution! Ja, Herr Hauptmann,

mysteriously

you might well have an apoplexia	Sie können eine apoplexia

like a donkey

cerebri any day; you possibly might have it just along the one side of your body. Yes! You'll probably find you're [only] paralysed on one side perhaps,	cerebri kriegen; Sie können sie aber vielleicht nur auf der einen Seite bekommen. Ja! Sie können auch [nur] auf der einen Seite gelähmt werden,

again very mysteriously

or with the best of luck, down there!	oder im besten Fall nur unten!

CAPTAIN
groaning

Oh, heavens!	Um Gottes —

DOCTOR
in full swing

Yes! That could be just about your own prospects throughout the coming four weeks now. All the same I'd like to assure you that the progress of your illness surely will be most fascinating and if God wills your tongue be paralysed even partly, then we shall do the most immortal experimenting.	Ja! Das sind so ungefähr Ihre Aussichten auf die nächsten vier Wochen! Übrigens kann ich Sie versichern, dass Sie einen von den intressanten Fällen abgeben werden und wenn Gott will, dass Ihre Zunge zum Teil gelähmt wird, so machen wir die unsterblichsten Experimente.

The Captain grasps at the Doctor and holds him firm. The Doctor tries to escape from his grasp.

CAPTAIN

Stop, Doctor! I won't let you go! Grave-digger Death's old friend! Within four weeks?	Halt, Doktor! Ich lasse Sie nicht! Sargnagel! Totenfreund! In vier Wochen?

quite out of breath

There are some people who die of shock . . . Doctor!	Es sind schon Leute am puren Schreck . . . Doktor!

84

He coughs with excitement and exertion, takes several deep breaths, the Doctor tapping him on the back. He coughs less and less.

with emotion

Right now I see the mourners with their handkerchiefs at their faces.	Ich sehe schon die Leute mit den Sacktüchern vor den Augen[1].

[1]with even more emotion

And they will all be saying: he was a worthy man. a worthy man —	Aber sie werden sagen: Er war ein guter Mensch, ein guter Mensch —

DOCTOR

waving his hat and pretending to have only just noticed him

[Well, I never! Good morning, Captain!	[Ei! guten Morgen, Herr Hauptmann!

holding out his hat

What's that? That, Captain, is an empty head!	Was ist das? Herr Hauptmann, das ist — Hohlkopf!

CAPTAIN

making a crease in his coat

[And what's that, my good Doctor? There you can see simple-mindedness on the increase! Ha ha ha! No offence, mind. I'm a good person really, but I can give as good as I get when I want to —]	[Und was ist das, Herr Doctor? Das ist Einfalt! Hahaha! Aber nichts für ungut! Ich bin ein guter Mensch, aber ich kann auch, wenn ich will! Herr Doctor, ich sag' Ihnen, wenn ich will —]

The Doctor, deeply moved and trying to distract the Captain, sees Wozzeck. Wozzeck salutes as he hastens past.

DOCTOR [2]

Hey, Wozzeck!	He, Wozzeck!

Wozzeck stops. [11]

Why hurry so fast and pass us by?	Was hetzt Er sich so an uns vorbei?

Wozzeck salutes and starts off again, but then decides to stay, and comes back slowly.

Stay a while, Wozzeck!	Bleib Er doch, Wozzeck!

CAPTAIN

calming down again; to Wozzeck

You run by like an open knife, a razor slicing the world; we cut ourselves on you!	Er läuft ja wie ein offenes Rasiermesser durch die Welt, man schneidet sich an Ihm!

The Captain looks closer at Wozzeck, who stands there dumb and earnest, then he turns somewhat ashamed to the Doctor and continues with a reference to his beard.

---

1. mit den Citronen in den Händen — with lemons in their hands (an old German funeral custom).
2. Berg divided this speech between the Doctor and the Captain. 'Katzenschweife' is a misreading for 'Kastrirte' — eunuchs.

Wozzeck rushes past, saluting them.

CAPTAIN

Hey! Wozzeck! Where are you rushing off to then? Stay and talk for a moment! You go through the world like an open razor. Somebody'll cut themselves on you. You're running so fast, it's as though you had to shave a whole regiment of cats' tails and would be hanged if you missed a single hair — but talking of hair — what was I going to say — long beards —	He! Wozzeck! Was hetzt Er sich so an uns vorbei? Bleib Er doch, Wozzeck! Er läuft ja wie ein offenes Rasirmesser durch die Welt, man schneidet sich an Ihm! Er läuft, als hätte er ein Regiment Katzenschweife zu rasiren, und würde gehenkt, so lange noch ein letztes Haar — aber über die langen Bärte — was wollte ich doch sagen — die langen Bärte —

You run as if all the whiskers of the Varsity professors needed shaving, and you would be hanged, so long as a single hair . . . Exactly.	Er läuft, als hätt Er die Vollbärte aller Universitäten zu rasieren, und würde gehängt, so lang noch ein letztes Haar . . . Ja richtig.

[1]
whistling

Those fine long beards, yes (what was it I was saying?)	Die langen Bärte . . . (was wollte ich doch sagen?)

He whistles as he thinks.

those fine long beards, what?	die langen Bärte —

DOCTOR
quoting [8]

'A fine long beard beneath the chin' (hmm!), the Romans wrote of that,	'Ein langer Bart unter dem Kinn' (hm!), schon Plinius spricht davon,

The Captain realises the Doctor's allusion and taps his forehead.

one ought to stop . . .	man muss ihn[1] den . . .

CAPTAIN

Ha!	Ha!

DOCTOR

. . . those soldiers wearing beards —	. . . Soldaten abgewöhnen —

CAPTAIN
tapping his forehead

While the Captain is speaking, the Doctor listens with considerable amusement, humming his theme, and beating time with his stick as if it were the Drum Major's stick.

That's it,	Ich habs,

very significantly

[Ha,] those fine long beards, yes! Well then, Wozzeck? Did you find a hair from such a beard inside your bowl at breakfast? Ha-ha! Do you see my point?	[Ha,] die langen Bärte! Was ist's Wozzeck? Hat Er nicht ein Haar aus einem Bart in seiner Schüssel gefunden? Ha ha! Er versteht mich doch?

The Doctor is humming.

A hair from a certain person, the beard of a recruit, or some junior officer we know,	Ein Haar von einem Menschen, vom Bart eines Sappeurs, oder eines Unteroffiziers,

The Doctor continues to hum.

or else of some Drum Major, perhaps.	oder eines Tambourmajors.

DOCTOR
humming

Hey, Wozzeck? Nevertheless, you've a faithful wife? [Hey?]	He, Wozzeck? Aber Er hat doch ein braves Weib?! [he?]

WOZZECK

[Yes!] But what do you mean by that, Sir, good Doctor, and what . . .	[Ja wohl!] Was wollen Sie damit sagen, Herr Doktor, und Sie,

to the Captain

do you, Sir?!	Herr Hauptmann?!

CAPTAIN

What a face the fellow's pulling! Well! So you found none in your breakfast, but if you were to run around the corner there, then it is quite likely you'd find upon two lips there lying a hair — namely! Yes, indeed, on two lips! [Wozzeck, a pair of lips!] Yes! I too have	Was der Kerl für ein Gesicht macht! Nun! wenn auch nicht grad in der Suppe, aber wenn Er sich eilt und um die Ecke läuft[2], so kann Er vielleicht noch auf einem Paar Lippen eins finden! Ein Haar — nämlich! Übrigens, ein Paar Lippen! [Wozzeck, ein paar Lippen!] O!

---

1. man muss es dem Soldaten abgewöhnen — You have to stop soldiers doing it. 2. geht — go to

known the pleasure that love can bestow! But what's this, man? Your face is white as chalk!	Ich habe auch einmal die Liebe gefühlt! Aber, Kerl, Er ist ja kreideweiss!

WOZZECK

~~Maybe, Sir, I am a simple fellow!~~ In this world she's all I have! But, Captain, if you joke with me —	Herr Hauptmann, ich bin ein armer Teufel! Hab' sonst nichts auf dieser[1] Welt! Herr Hauptmann, wenn Sie Spass machen —

CAPTAIN
flaring up

Joke?! I? Whatever . . .? Joke! Fellow . . .	Spass?! Ich? Dass Dich der . . . Spass! Kerl . . .

DOCTOR

[Your pulse, Wozzeck! Short, violent, racing —]	[Den Puls, Wozzeck! Klein, hart, hüpfend —]

WOZZECK

But Captain, for me the world is hot as hell and hell is so cold against it, Sir . . .	Herr Hauptmann, die Erd' ist manchem höllenheiss, die Hölle ist kalt dagegen, Herr . . .

CAPTAIN

Fellow, don't get suicidal! You're stabbing me with eyes like daggers!	Kerl, will Er sich erschiessen? Er sticht mich ja mit seinen Augen!

DOCTOR

Your pulse, Wozzeck!	Den Puls, Wozzeck!

He feels his pulse.

Short . . . hard . . . arhythmic —	Klein . . . hart . . . arhythmisch — [2]

WOZZECK

Oh, please, Sir . . .	Herr Hauptmann . . .

He snatches his hand away from the Doctor.

CAPTAIN

I mean well by you, for you're a worthy fellow, Wozzeck,	Ich mein's gut mit Ihm, weil Er ein guter Mensch ist, Wozzeck,

with emotion

a worthy man!	ein guter Mensch!

WOZZECK [3]
to himself, but getting louder

There's much that's likely . . For man . . . There's much that's likely . . .	Es ist viel möglich . . . Der Mensch . . . Es ist viel möglich . . .

DOCTOR
looking at Wozzeck enquiringly

And face muscles stiff, and taut stony stare.	Gesichtsmuskeln starr, gespannt, Augen stier.

WOZZECK

God in Heaven! One could be really tempted to hang oneself! Then one would know just where one is!	Gott im Himmel! Man könnte Lust bekommen, sich aufzuhängen! Dann wüsste man, woran man ist!

He rushes off without taking leave. The Captain, puzzled, follows Wozzeck with his eyes.

---

1. Der Welt! 2. Büchner's order of lines in this scene is slightly different.
3. Büchner closes the scene differently; see overleaf, note 2.

How the fellow runs, and his shadow in pursuit!

Wie der Kerl läuft und sein Schatten hinterdrein!

DOCTOR

A real phenomenon, this man Wozzeck!

Er ist ein Phänomen, dieser Wozzeck!

CAPTAIN

These human creatures make me giddy! It's most confusing! This won't do at all!

Mir wird ganz schwindlich vor[1] dem Menschen! Und wie verzweifelt! Das hab ich nicht gern!

[1]

He joins the Doctor, who, fearing a new emotional outburst from the Captain, has begun to move off, as if suddenly remembering his haste at the beginning of the scene.

A worthy man is grateful unto God; a worthy man has no need to be brave! Only scoundrels must be brave!

Ein guter Mensch ist dankbar gegen Gott; ein guter Mensch hat auch keine Courage! Nur ein Hundsfott hat Courage!

moving off

Only a scoundrel . . .

Nur ein Hundsfott! . . .

behind the scene

Scoundrels . . .

Hundsfott . . .

Curtain.[2]

Change of scene.

---

1. von dem Menschen
2. Büchner's end of scene (see previous page, note 3):

WOZZECK

I'm going — anything's possible! Human beings! — anything's possible! Yes or no? God in Heaven! Don't you just feel like driving a peg into it and hanging yourself from it? Then you'd know where you were! Yes or no?

Ich geh' — es ist viel möglich! Der Mensch — es ist viel möglich! Ja oder nein? Gott im Himmel! Man könnt' Lust bekommen, einen Kloben hineinzuschlagen und sich dran aufzuhängen. Dann wüsst' man, woran man ist! Ja oder nein?

He runs away.

DOCTOR

Quite a phenomenon, that Wozzeck!

Er ist ein Phänomen, dieser Wozzeck!

CAPTAIN

He makes me feel quite giddy! Just look at the beanpole running away, with his shadow in hot pursuit! And so desperate! I don't like it! A good person is grateful to God. And a good person doesn't show courage! Only a scoundrel shows courage! I sometimes feel depressed, too; there's a certain effusiveness to my character, I can't stop crying when I see my coat hanging on the wall! But man exists to praise his creator and fortify himself in his love of life. Only a scoundrel shows courage! Only a scoundrel!

Mir wird ganz schwindlig von dem Menschen! Wie der lange Schlingel läuft und sein Schatten hinterdrein! und so verzweifelt! Das hab ich nicht gerne! Ein guter Mensch ist dankbar gegen Gott. Ein guter Mensch hat auch keine Courage! Nur ein Hundsfott hat Courage! Ich bin auch manchmal schwermütig; ich hab' in meiner Natur so was Schwärmerisches, ich muss immer weinen, wenn ich meinen Rock an der Wand hängen sehe! Aber der Mensch ist dazu da, um seinen Schöpfer zu preisen und sich in der Liebe zum Leben zu befestigen. Nur ein Hundsfott hat Courage! Nur ein Hundsfott.

Scene Three. *The street before Marie's dwelling. A dull day. Marie stands outside her door. Wozzeck comes rushing up to her. [·*

MARIE
spoken

Good morning, Franz.	Guten Tag, Franz.

WOZZECK
staring at her and shaking his head
spoken

I see nothing, I see nothing. If one could see, and could hold it firmly in one's grasp!	Ich seh' nichts, ich seh' nichts. O, man müsst's seh'n, man müsst's greifen können mit den Fäusten!

MARIE

What's wrong, Franz?	Was hast, Franz?

WOZZECK

It's still you, Marie? Such a sin, so gross and rank, should be smelling to highest heaven and driving the angels away. But, see, you have such fine red lips, [Marie,] such fine red lips — and no blister there?	Bist Du's noch, Marie?! Eine Sünde, so dick und breit das müsst' stinken, dass man die Engel[chen] zum Himmel hinausräuchern könnt'. Aber Du hast einen roten Mund, [Marie!] einen roten Mund — keine Blase drauf?

MARIE

Your mind's wandering, Franz. I'm frightened . . .	Du bist hirnwütig, Franz. Ich fürcht' mich . . .

WOZZECK
with some voice

You are fair —	Du bist schön —

singing

'fair as sin is'.	'wie die Sünde'.

spoken again

How, then, can a mortal sin be so fair, Marie?	Aber kann die Todsünde so schön sein, Marie?

He points suddenly to a place by the door.
flaring up

Here! Was it here you saw him? Here, here?	[4,9] Da! Hat er da gestanden, so, so?

MARIE

It is not my street if people want to stand there . . .	[10] Ich kann den Leuten die Gasse nicht verbieten . . .

WOZZECK

Devil! Was it there you saw him?	Teufel! Hat er da gestanden?

MARIE

Just as the day's long and the world ancient, many people can stand all in the same place, one after the other.	Dieweil der Tag lang und die Welt alt ist, können viele Menschen an einem Platze stehn, einer nach dem andern.

WOZZECK

I saw him, I say!	Ich hab ihn gesehn!

MARIE

You can see much, if you have eyes to see,	Man kann viel sehn, wenn man zwei Augen hat,

Wozzeck is losing control more and more.

and if you're not blind, and if the sun shines.	und wenn man nicht blind ist, und wenn die Sonne scheint.

89

WOZZECK
breaking out

You — with him! / Du — bei ihm!

MARIE

What of it! / Und wenn auch!

WOZZECK

Bitch! / Mensch!

He rushes at her.

MARIE

Keep your hands off! / Rühr' mich nicht an.

Wozzeck slowly drops his hand.

Better a knife-blade in my heart, than lay a hand on me. / [12] Lieber ein Messer in den Leib, als eine Hand auf mich.

moving off

My father did not dare to when I was ten years old . . . / Mein Vater hats nicht gewagt, wie ich zehn Jahr alt war . . .

She goes into the house. Wozzeck stands staring at her.

WOZZECK

'Better a knife-blade' . . . / [12] 'Lieber ein Messer' . . .

in a frightened whisper

Ah! Man is a chasm. It makes you giddy when you look down inside . . . / Der Mensch ist ein Abgrund, es schwindelt Einem, wenn man hinunter schaut . . .

going off stage

Yes, giddy . . . / mich schwindelt . . .

Slow curtain.

Change of scene (to Scene Four).

The next scene is not in the libretto.

Guardroom. *Wozzeck and Andres.*

ANDRES
singing

The landlord's wife has a pretty maid,
She sits in the garden day and night,
She sits there in the garden —

/ Frau Wirthin hat eine brave Magd,
Sie sitzt im Garten Tag und Nacht,
Sie sitzt in ihrem Garten —

WOZZECK

Andres! / Andres!

ANDRES

Well? / Nu!

WOZZECK

Where do you think she . . . Nice weather! / Was meinst, wo sie . . . Schön Wetter!

ANDRES

Sunday weather! Music outside the town! The womenfolk have set off already . . . dancing . . . the lads sweating . . . great! / Sonntagswetter! Musik vor der Stadt. Vorhin sind die Weibsbilder hin . . . Tanz . . . die Bursche dampfen, das geht!

WOZZECK
uneasily

Dancing, Andres, they're dancing! / Tanz, Andres, sie tanzen!

ANDRES

At The Horse and The Star.	Im Rössl und im Stern.

WOZZECK

Where do you think she — I've got to see where they're dancing!	Was glaubst, wo sie — ich muss sehen, wo sie tanzen!

ANDRES

As you like.	Meinetwegen.

singing

She sits there in the garden, Until the clock strikes twelve, Waiting for the soldiers.	Sie sitzt im ihrem Garten, Bis dass das Glöcklein zwölfe schlägt, Und passt auf die Soldaten.

WOZZECK

Andres, I can't get any peace.	Andres, ich hab keine Ruh.

ANDRES

More fool you!	Narr!

WOZZECK

I've got to get out. Everything's spinning before my eyes. Dancing. She'll be hot! Dammit! — I'm off!	Ich muss hinaus. Es dreht sich mir vor den Augen. Tanz! Wird sie heiss haben! Verdammt! — Adies!

ANDRES

What's the matter?	Was willst du?

WOZZECK

I have to go, see for myself.	Ich muss fort, muss sehen.

ANDRES

Because of that slut?	Wegen dem Mensch!

WOZZECK

Got to get out, got to get out!	Hinaus, hinaus!

The curtain rises slowly.

Scene Four. *Tavern garden. Late evening. Apprentices, soldiers and serving girls; some are dancing, others watching.*

FIRST APPRENTICE

I've got a shirt on but it is not mine,	Ich hab' ein Hemdlein an, das ist nicht mein,

SECOND APPRENTICE

imitating the First Apprentice

It is not mine ... [Forget me not! Friendship! Brother, shall I punch a hole in nature out of friendship. Brother! I intend to make a hole in you. I'll kill every flea on your body. Brother, I'm a man as well, you know.]	Das ist nicht mein ... [Vergissmeinnicht! Freundschaft! Bruder, soll ich dir aus Freundschaft ein Loch in die Natur machen? Bruder! ich will ein Loch in deine Natur machen, ich will dir alle Flöh' am Leib totschlagen. Bruder, ich bin auch ein Kerl, du weisst —]

FIRST APPRENTICE

As for my soul, it stinks of brandy and wine.	Und meine Seele stinkt nach Branntewein.

Apprentices, soldiers and girls move in a leisurely way from the dance floor, and gather in groups, one group around the drunken apprentices.

My soul, my own immortal soul, stinks of brandy and wine! It stinks, and I do	Meine Seele, meine unsterbliche Seele, stinket nach Branntewein! Sie stinket,

not know why! Wherefore is the world so sad? Even money turns into corruption! [Let the devil take the dear God! Brother, I feel like weeping a vat full of tears.]

und ich weiss nicht, warum? Warum ist die Welt so traurig? Selbst das Geld geht in Verwesung über! [Der Teufel soll den lieben Herrgott holen! Bruder, ich muss ein Regenfass voll greinen.]

SECOND APPRENTICE

Forget me not! Brother! Friendship!

Vergiss mein nicht! Bruder! Freundschaft!

embracing him

Wherefore is the world so happy! I wish that our noses could be two full bottles, and that we could pour them into each other's gullets. The whole wide world is rosy red! Brandy, that is my life-blood!

Warum ist die Welt so schön! Ich wollt', unsre Nasen wären zwei Bouteillen, und wir könnten sie uns einander in den Hals giessen. Die ganze Welt ist rosenrot! Branntewein, das ist mein[1] Leben!

FIRST APPRENTICE

My soul, my own immortal soul stinks. Oh! [I'm in my own way and have to jump over myself!] That is sad, sad, sad, sad . . .

Meine Seele,[2] meine unsterbliche Seele stinket. Oh! [ich lieg mir selbst im Weg und muss über mich springen!] Das ist traurig, traurig, traurig, trau . . .

He falls asleep. The company returns to the dance floor and begins to dance. Amongst them, Marie and the Drum Major. Wozzeck rushes on and sees Marie dancing past with the Drum Major.

WOZZECK
spoken

Him! Her! The Devil!

Er! Sie! Teufel!

MARIE
dancing past, singing

On we go, on we go!

Immer zu, immer zu!

WOZZECK
still spoken

'On we go, on we go!' [on we go!]

[9, 10] 'Immer zu, immer zu!' [Immer zu!]

Wozzeck sits on the bench near the dance-floor.

Twisting, turning! Why doesn't God put out the sun now?

Dreht Euch! Wälzt Euch! Warum löscht Gott die Sonne nicht aus?

still spoken

Everything twists and turns in lust: man and woman, beast with beast! [They do it in broad daylight, they do it on one's hands, like midges.]

Alles wälzt sich in Unzucht über einander: Mann und Weib, Mensch und Vieh! [Sie thun's am hellen Tag, sie thun's schier einem auf den Händen, wie die Mücken.]

He looks again at the dance-floor.

spoken

Women! Women! . . . Women are like fire! Fire! Fire! . . .

Weib! Weib! . . . Das Weib ist heiss! ist heiss! heiss! . . .[3]

He jumps up violently.

How he mauls her with his hands! Touches her body! And she just laughs! . . .

[9] Wie er an ihr herumgreift! An ihrem Leib! Und sie lacht dazu! . . .

MARIE
amongst the dancers

On we go! On we go!

Immer zu! Immer zu!

DRUM MAJOR

On we go!

Immer zu!

---

1. ein Leben — a life 2. phrase added by Berg 3. Berg added this exclamation.

On we go!

Wozzeck is getting more and more excited.

Immer zu!

Wozzeck is unable to control himself.

WOZZECK
spoken

Damn!   Verdammt!

He is about to rush on to the dance-floor, but the dance finishes and the company leaves the floor.

I...   Ich...

Wozzeck sits down again.

APPRENTICES AND SOLDIERS

A hunter from the South	Ein Jäger aus der Pfalz
was riding through a shady grove!	Ritt einst durch einen grünen Wald!
Halli, Hallo! Halli, Hallo!	Halli, Hallo! Halli, Hallo!
Oh, happy is the hunter's life,	Ja lustig ist die Jägerei,
from morning unto night! ✗	Allhie auf grüner Haid!
Halli, Hallo! Halli, Hallo!	Halli, Hallo! Halli, Hallo!

Andres, seizing the guitar, sets himself up as a chorus conductor and gives a final ritardando, so that he can come in with the last chord of the chorus as it dies away.

ANDRES

Oh daughter, dearest daughter,	O Tochter, liebe Tochter,
what had you in mind	Was hast Du gedacht,
when flirting with the coachman	Dass Du dich an die Kutscher
and the stable boys in bed?! ✗	Und die Fuhrknecht hast gehängt?!
... Hallo!	... Hallo![1]

APPRENTICES AND SOLDIERS

Oh, happy is the hunter's life	Ja lustig ist die Jägerei
from morning unto night!	Allhie auf grüner Haid!
Halli, Hallo! Halli, Hallo!	Halli, Hallo! Halli, Hallo!

ANDRES

Hallo!   Hallo!

He gives the guitar back to the player in the band and then turns to Wozzeck.

OTHER APPRENTICES
singing

[Oh daughter, daughter of my flesh —	[O Tochter, meine Tochter —
What was she thinking of? What fresh	Was hat sie gedacht,
Idea made her try the joys	Dass sie sich an die Kutscher
Of coachmen and of cabin-boys?]	Und die Schiffsleut' hat gehängt?!]

A SOLDIER[2]
to Wozzeck

[What are you doing?]   [Was machst du?]

WOZZECK

What's the time?   Wie viel Uhr?

ANDRES [2]

Eleven!   Elf Uhr!

WOZZECK

Eh? I thought it was later still! The time	So? Ich meint', es müsst später sein! Die
goes very slow at these parties —	Zeit wird Einem lang bei der Kurzweil —

---

1. Exclamation interpolated by Berg. 2. A 'soldier' becomes Andres according to Berg.

Why sit like that, so near the door?

Was sitzest Du da vor der Tür?

WOZZECK

I'm alright here. Many people sit near to the door and do not know it till they are carried out through the door feet first!

Ich sitz' gut da. Es sind manche Leut' mah an der Tür und wissen's nicht, bis [12] man sie zur Tür hinausträgt, die Füss' voran!

ANDRES

Why sit alone?

Du sitzest hart.

WOZZECK

No matter, and in coolest grave there I will lie still better.

Gut sitz' ich, und im kühlen Grab da lieg' ich dann noch besser.

The dance ends. Apprentices, soldiers and girls leave the dance-floor and are turning to the First Apprentice. Andres is bored. He whistles to himself and, thinking more of dancing, he turns away from Wozzeck.

ANDRES

Are you drunk, Franz . . .?

Bist besoffen . . .?

He whistles.

WOZZECK

Me, drunk, Andres? No such luck!

Nein, leider, bring's nit z'sam.

He remains alone on the bench. Meanwhile the First Apprentice has revived. He climbs onto a table and begins to preach to the accompaniment of the stage band.

FIRST APPRENTICE

And yet, if a wanderer, who is leaning on the stream of time, suddenly should have a vision of God in majestic wisdom and asketh: Wherefore, then, is man?

Jedoch, wenn ein Wanderer, der gelehnt steht an dem Strom der Zeit, oder aber sich die göttliche Weisheit vergegenwärtigt[1] und fraget: Warum ist der Mensch?

with feeling

And yet, verily, verily, brethren, I say to you:

Aber wahrlich, geliebte Zuhörer, ich sage Euch:

ecstatic

It is good so! For from what should then the farmer, the caskmaker, the tailor, the quack, earn their living, if God had not created human beings? From what should then the tailor earn his living, if God had not first in man implanted a strong sense of shame at his nakedness? From what should the soldier and host live, if God hadn't given man the need to shoot and kill people, and if parching thirst were not always our lot? Therefore, beloved, do not doubt, for it is all so lovely and fine . . . Know that all is vanity that's worldly; even money turns into corruption. As for my [immortal] soul, it [very much] stinks of brandy and wine. [Finally, ladies and gentlemen, let's piss on the Cross so that another Jew will die!]

Es ist gut so! Denn von was hätten der Landmann, der Fassbinder, der Schneider, der Arzt leben sollen, wenn Gott den Menschen nicht geschaffen hätte? Von was hätte der Schneider leben sollen, wenn Er nicht dem Menschen die Empfindung der Schamhaftigkeit eingepflanzt hätte? Von was der Soldat und der Wirt, wenn Er ihn nicht mit dem Bedürfnis des Totschiessens[2] und der Feuchtigkeit ausgerüstet hätte? Darum, Geliebteste, zweifelt nicht; denn es ist Alles lieblich und fein . . . Aber alles Irdische ist eitel; selbst das Geld geht in Verwesung über, und meine [unsterbliche] Seele stinkt [sehr] nach Branntewein. [Zum Schluss, meine geliebten Zuhörer, lasset uns noch über's Kreuz p—n, damit ein Jud stirbt!]

---

1. beantwortet — answered 2. Todtschlagens — the need to kill

[She's got red cheeks, and he's got a beautiful beard! Why not? Why not indeed!]

[Sie hat rothe Backen, und er einen schönen Bart! Warum nicht? Warum also nicht?]

There is general uproar. The speaker is surrounded and carried away by some of the apprentices. The others return singing to the dance-floor or to the tables.

SOLDIERS AND APPRENTICES

Oh, happy is the hunter's life . . . Halli!

Ja lustig ist die Jägerei . . . Halli!

ANDRES
going up-stage

Oh, daughter, dearest daughter . . .

O Tochter, liebe Tochter . . .

The Idiot suddenly appears, and creeps up to Wozzeck, who is still sitting on the bench, having taken no part in the preceding action. As the band begin to tune their instruments, the Idiot presses closer to Wozzeck.

THE IDIOT
close to Wozzeck

Happy, happy . . .

Lustig, lustig . . .

Wozzeck does not notice the Idiot at first.
craftily

And yet it smells.

aber es riecht.

WOZZECK

Fool, what is it?

Narr, was willst Du?

THE IDIOT

I smell, I smell blood!

Ich riech, ich riech Blut!

WOZZECK

Blood? Blood, Blood!

Blut? Blut, Blut!

Apprentices, soldiers and girls, amongst them Marie and the Drum Major, again begin to dance.

WOZZECK

There's a red mist before me. They all seem twisting and then rolling [in a sea of blood] over each other . . .

Mir wird rot vor den Augen. Mir ist, als wälzten sie sich alle [in einem Meer von Blut] über einander . . .

The curtain falls quickly.

Change of scene (to Scene Five.) *The curtain rises slowly.*

The next scene is not in the libretto.

Open field. Night.

WOZZECK

On and on! On and on! Stop the music! Ha! What did you say? So — louder! louder! I can hear it now. Stab — stab the she-wolf dead — Stab — stab — the she-wolf dead — shall I? — must I? — I can still hear it, on and on — stab her dead — dead — it's coming from down there under the ground, and the poplars are saying it — stab her dead — stab her —

Immer zu! Immer zu! Still Musik! Ha! was sagt Ihr? So — lauter! lauter! Jetzt hör' ich's. Stich — stich — die Zickwölfin todt — stich — stich — die Zickwölfin todt — soll ich? — muss ich? — Ich hör's immer, immer zu — stich todt — todt — Da unten aus dem Boden heraus spricht's, und die Pappeln sprechen's — stich todt — stich —

Scene Five. *A guardroom in the barracks.* Night. *A chorus of sleeping soldiers is heard as the curtain rises. Andres is lying with Wozzeck on a wooden bed, sleeping.*

WOZZECK
moaning in his sleep

Oh, oh.   Oh, oh.
starting up

Andres! Andres! I cannot sleep.   Andres! Andres! Ich kann nicht schlafen.

The soldiers, who are sleeping on wooden beds, rouse slightly at Wozzeck's words, but do not become fully awake.

Each time I close my eyelids, I see them still quite clearly, and I hear the fiddlers, on we go, on we go. And the walls seem to speak to me.	Wenn ich die Augen zumach', dann seh' ich sie doch immer, und ich hör' die Geigen immerzu, immerzu. Und dann spricht's aus der Wand heraus.

getting excited

Can't you hear, Andres? How they play and dance?!	Hörst Du nix, Andres? Wie das geigt und springt?!

ANDRES
sleepy

[Yes!] Let them dance then . . .   [Ja!] Lass sie tanzen . . .

WOZZECK

And between there is a flashing all the time, just like a knife-blade, like a glittering knife-blade! [And soon it will lie on a table in a shop in a dark alleyway, and soon I'll have it in my hand, and — oh!]	Und dazwischen blitzt immer vor den Augen wie ein Messer, wie ein breites [12] Messer! [und bald liegt's auf einem Tisch in einem Laden in einer dunkler. Gass', und bald hab' ich's in der Hand und — oh!]

ANDRES

Sleep, fool!   Schlaf, Narr!

WOZZECK

My Lord and God,   Mein Herr und Gott,
praying

'and lead us not into temptation, Amen!'   'und führe uns nicht in Versuchung, Amen!'

DRUM MAJOR
entering noisily, very drunk

I am a man! I have a woman, I tell you, a woman! To breed Drum Majors like me! Her bosom, her thighs, are all so firm! Her eyes were like coals hot and glowing. I have a woman, I tell you . . .	[9] Ich bin ein Mann! Ich hab' ein Weibsbild, ich sag' Ihm, ein Weibsbild! Zur Zucht von Tambourmajors! Ein Busen und Schenkel! Und alles fest! Die Augen wie glühende Kohlen. Kurzum[1] ein Weibsbild, ich sag' Ihm . . .

ANDRES

Hey! Who is it, then?   He! Wer ist es denn?

DRUM MAJOR

Ask that man Wozzeck, there! [Ha ha! I am a man, a man!][2]	[2] Frag' Er den Wozzeck da! [Hehe! Ich bin ein Mann, ein Mann!][2]

---

1. 'Kurzum' — added by Berg

2. There are two versions of the rest of this scene according to the 1909 Landau edition. The one which Berg followed is our main text, while the other is given on page 99 (see Kenneth Segar's article).

96

Above: Hermann Winkler (Drum Major) and Walter Berry (Wozzeck), Cologne, 1975; production by Hans Neugebauer with designs by Achim Freyer (photo: Archiv Universal Edition). Below: William Lewis (Drum Major) and Benjamin Luxon (Wozzeck), Scottish Opera, 1983 (photo: Eric Thorburn)

He pulls a bottle of brandy from his pocket, drinks from it and hands it to Wozzeck.

There, man, drink. I wish the world   Da Kerl, sauf'. Ich wollt', die Welt wär
were drunk, drunk, for men must drink!   Schnaps, Schnaps, der Mann muss saufen!

He drinks again.

Drink, man, drink.   Sauf', Kerl, sauf'.

Wozzeck looks away and whistles.

very angry

Lout, shall I rip your tongue from your   Kerl, soll ich Dir die Zung' aus dem Hals
gullet and wrap it round your neck tightly?   zieh'n und sie Dir um den Leib wickeln?

The Drum Major and Wozzeck wrestle. Wozzeck is thrust to the ground.

Do you want as much breath inside   [2] Soll ich Dir noch so viel Atem lassen,
you . . .

He grasps Wozzeck firmly by the throat.

as an old woman's fart?   als ein (Altweiberfurz?)

bending over Wozzeck

Do you . . .   [2] Soll ich . . .

He lets go of Wozzeck, pulls himself up and takes the bottle from his pocket. Wozzeck sinks back exhausted.

Now let the lout whistle!   Jetzt soll der Kerl pfeifen!

He drinks again.

Black and blue, let him now whistle!   Dunkelblau, soll er sich pfeifen!

He whistles.

triumphantly

That's what I call a man!   [10] Was bin ich für ein Mann!

He turns and crashes out of the door, which slams after him. The scene without the Drum Major. Wozzeck has lifted himself slowly from the ground onto his bed.

A SOLDIER
pointing at Wozzeck

He had his fill!   Der hat sein Fett!

ANDRES

He's bleeding.   Er blut'.

The soldier turns over and goes to sleep.

WOZZECK

One after the other!   Einer nach dem Andern!

He remains seated, staring in front of him. The other soldiers, who had risen up on their beds during the fight, have all lain down and are sleeping again.

[11]

Laundau offers this scene as a variant of the above.

Exit Drum Major.

WOZZECK
to Andres

Did he talk about me? What did he say?

Er hat von mir geredt? Was hat er gesagt?

ANDRES

I was to ask you who his whore is. Said she was a fine figure of a woman — great thighs —

Ich sollt' dich fragen, wer sein Mensch ist. Hätt ein prächtig Weibsbild — die hätt' Schenkel —

WOZZECK
quite coldly

Really? Is that what he said? What do you think I dreamt about last night. Andres? — Wasn't it about a knife? — What stupid dreams people have! Or perhaps they're not so stupid?

So? Hat er das gesagt? Was hat mir heut Nacht geträumt, Andres? War's nicht von einem Messer? — Was man doch närrische Träume hat! Oder kluge Träume?

He prepares to leave.

ANDRES

Where are you off to, comrade?

Wohin, Kamerad?

WOZZECK

To fetch the Captain's wine. Oh, Andres, she was one in a million!

Meinem Hauptmann Wein holen. Ach! Andres, sie war doch ein einzig Mädel!

ANDRES

Who was? What do you mean, 'was'? Isn't she any more?

Wer war? War? Ist nicht mehr?

WOZZECK

Won't be soon. Bye!

Wird bald nicht mehr sein. Adies!

End of Act Two.

Act Three

Scene One. *Marie's room. It is night, candle-light. Marie, alone with her child, is sitting at the table, turning the pages of a Bible and reading. The child is nearby.*

MARIE
spoken

'And out of his mouth there came forth neither deceit nor falsehood ...'

'Und ist kein Betrug in seinem Munde erfunden worden ...'

singing

Lord God, Lord God! Look not on me!

Herr Gott, Herr Gott! Sieh mich nicht an!

She turns the pages and reads further.

spoken

'Wherefore the Pharisees had taken and brought to Him an adulterous woman [and set her in the midst].' 'Jesus said to her: Thus do I condemn you no more. Go forth, go forth in peace and sin no more.'

'Aber die Pharisäer brachten ein Weib zu ihm, so im Ehebruch lebte [und stelleten sie vor ihm].' 'Jesus aber sprach: So verdamme ich dich auch nicht, geh' hin, und sündige hinfort nicht mehr.'

sung

Lord God! [Lord! I can't — Lord! Give me strength enough to pray.]

Herr Gott! [Herrgott! — ich kann nicht — Herrgott! gieb mir nur so viel, dass ich beten kann.]

She covers her face with her hands. The child presses up to Marie.

The boy's looks really stab my heart. Be off!

Der Bub gibt mir einen Stich in's Herz. Fort!

pushing the child from her

My sin's clear as the daylight!

Das brüst' sich in der Sonne!

Ah no, come here!

suddenly more gentle

Nein komm, komm hier!

Come to me!

Komm zu mir![1]

beginning to tell the story, speaking

'And once there was a poor little mite, and he had no father nor any mother, for all were dead. There was no one in the world, so the boy went hungry and he wept day and night. And he had nobody left in the world ...'

'Es war einmal ein armes Kind und hatt' keinen Vater und keine Mutter, war Alles tot und war Niemand auf der Welt, und es hat gehungert und geweint Tag und Nacht. Und weil es Niemand mehr hatt' auf der Welt ...'

singing

But Franz did not come here yesterday or today ... [I'm getting hot, hot!]

Der Franz ist nit kommen, gestern nit, heut' nit ... [Mir wird heiss, heiss!]

She hastily turns pages of the Bible.

What is written here of Mary Magdalene?

Wie steht es geschrieben von der Magdalena?

reading, with some singing voice

'And falling on her knees before Him, and weeping, she kissed His feet and washed them, and washed them with her tears, anointing them with ointment ...'

'Und kniete hin zu seinen Füssen und weinte und küsste seine Füsse und netzte sie mit Tränen und salbte sie mit Salben ...'

She beats her breast.

Lord God! Could I anoint Thy feet with ointment ... Saviour, as Thou hadst mercy on her, have mercy now on me, Lord! ...

Heiland! ich möchte Dir die Füsse salben ... Heiland, Du hast Dich ihrer erbarmt, erbarme Dich auch meiner! ...

Slow curtain.

Change of scene (to Scene Two).

---

1. Berg's interpolation.

Hildegard Behrens as Marie, Metropolitan Opera, 1989 (photo: Winnie Klotz)

The next three scenes are not in the libretto.

Junk shop. *Wozzeck. A Jew.*

WOZZECK

The pistol's too much.	Das Pistölchen ist zu theuer.

JEW

Well, are you going to buy it or not? It's not rubbish! What else is there?	Nu, kauft's nur — gaude Waar'! Kauft's nit? Was anders?

WOZZECK

What's the knife cost?	Was kost' das Messer?

JEW

Two florins! It's good! A good knife! You want to cut your throat with it? Well, what about it? I'm giving it away — you'll not find it cheaper anywhere else! You'll have a cheap death, but not a free one. You're going to buy it? Well?	Zwei Gulden! 'Sist gaud! a gaud's Messer. Wollt Ihr Euch den Hals mit abschneiden? Nun, was is? Ich geb's Euch so wohlfeil wie ein Anderer! Ihr sollt Euren Tod wohlfeil haben, aber doch nicht umsonst. Ihr kauft's? Nu?

WOZZECK

It'll cut more than bread —	Das kann mehr als Brod schneiden —

JEW

Yes, Sir!	Ja, Herrche!

WOZZECK

There!	Da!

He throws him the money, takes the knife and leaves.

JEW

There! Hihi! As if it was nothing! But it's money, after all. Hihi.	Da! Hihi! Als ob's nix wär! Und s'is doch Geld. Hihi.

Street. Sunday afternoon. *Marie by the front door, her child on her arm. An old woman next to her. Children playing in the street.*

LITTLE GIRLS
walking in pairs and singing

Brightly shines the sun today, Corn is growing too! Off they went across the lea, Walking two by two. Pipers to the fore, Fiddlers at the rear, Red shoes on their feet, On and on they went.	Wie heute schön die Sonne scheint, Wie steht das Korn im Blüh'n! Sie gingen über die Wiese hin, Sie gingen zwei und zwei. Die Pfeifer gingen vorne, Die Geiger hinterdrein, Sie hatten alle rothe Schuh Und gingen immer zu.

FIRST GIRL
stepping forward

Something else!	Was Anderes!

ALL

What else! What?	Was Anderes! Was?

FIRST GIRL

I don't know. Something else!	Ich weiss nit. Was Anderes!

MARIE

Come on — stand in a circle.	Kommt — alle im Kreis.

Singing, the children join in and move in a circle.

Ring-a-ring-a-roses, A pocketful of posies.	Ringel, Ringel, Rosenkranz, Ringel, Ringel!

FIRST GIRL

to the old woman

Grandma, why's the sun shining today?

Grossmutter, warum scheint heute die Sonn'?

OLD WOMAN

Because.

Darum!

FIRST GIRL

Why because?

Aber warum — darum?

SECOND GIRL

Tell us a story, Grandma.

Grossmutter, erzählt was!

MARIE

Yes, tell us a story, Auntie.

Ja, erzählt was Base.

OLD WOMAN

Once upon a time, there was a poor little boy who had neither father nor mother — they were all dead and there was no one left in the world, and he became hungry and cried day and night. And since there was no one left on earth, he decided to go to heaven. And the moon looked down on him like a friend, but when he finally got to the moon, it was a lump of rotten wood. And so he decided to go to the sun, and the sun looked down on him like a friend, but when he finally got to the sun, it was a withered sunflower. And so he decided to go to the stars, and the stars looked down on him like a friend, but when he finally got to the stars, they were golden midges skewered on blackthorns and dying. And so the boy decided to come back to earth, but when he got back to earth, the earth was an upturned pot. And so the boy was all alone, and he sat down and cried: 'I've no father or mother, no sun, moon or stars, and no earth.' And he's still sitting there, all alone.

Es war einmal ein arm Kind und hatt' keinen Vater und keine Mutter — war alles todt und war niemand auf der Welt, und es hat gehungert und geweint Tag und Nacht. Und weil es niemand mehr hatt' auf der Welt, wollt's in den Himmel geh'n. Und der Mond guckt' es so freundlich an, und wie's endlich zum Mond kommt, ist's ein Stück faul Holz. Da wollt's zur Sonne geh'n, und die Sonn' guckt' es so freundlich an, und wie's endlich zur Sonne kommt, ist's ein verwelkt Sonnblümlein. Da wollt's zu den Sternen geh'n, und die Sterne gucken es so freundlich an, und wie's endlich zu den Sternen kommt, da sind's goldene Mücklein, die sind auf gespiesst auf Schlehendörner und sterben. Da wollt' das Kind wieder zur Erde, aber wie's zur Erde kam, da war die Erde ein umgestürzt Häfchen. Und so war das Kind ganz allein und hat sich hingesetzt und hat geweint: Hab' nicht Vater noch Mutter, hab' nicht Sonne, Mond und Sterne und nicht die Erde. Und da sitzt es noch und ist ganz allein.

MARIE

pressing the child to her breast in fear

Ah, when I'm gone! Auntie, you make me sad at heart. My poor child! When I'm gone!

Ach! wenn ich todt bin! Bas', sie hat mir das Herz schwer gemacht. Mein armer Wurm! Wenn ich todt bin!

Barracks. *Andres. Wozzeck.*

WOZZECK

going through his kitbag

The nightshirt's not part of the kit. You might be able to use it, Andres! The crucifix belongs to my sister, so does the ring. I've also got two hearts, beautiful gold. My mother used to keep this here in her Bible, where it says,

Das Kamisölchen, Andres, gehört nit zur Montur. Du kannst's brauchen, Andres! Das Kreuz ist meiner Schwester und das Ringlein, ich hab' auch noch zwei Herzen, schön Gold. Das da lag in meiner Mutter Bibel, und da steht:

| Let suff'ring be my profit and my gain,
Oh let me dedicate my life to pain,
As your body, Lord, was red and wounded,
So let mine be till I, too, am dead. | Leiden sei all mein Gewinnst,
Leiden sei mein Gottesdienst,
Herr! wie Dein Leib war roth und wund,
So lass mein Herz sein alle Stund. |

ANDRES

completely motionless, looking at him bewildered, shaking his head, and saying to everything

| Yes. | Jawohl! |

WOZZECK

taking out a piece of paper

| Johann Franz Wozzeck, soldier and rifleman in the Second Regiment, Second Battalion, Fourth Company, born on the Feast of the Annunciation, 20 July. | Johann Franz Wozzeck, Wehrmann und Füselier im 2. Regiment, 2. Bataillon, 4. Compagnie, geboren Maria Verkündigung 20. Juli. |

He mutters the year.

| That makes me thirty years, seven months and twelve days old. | Ich bin heut alt 30 Jahr, 7 Monat und 12 Tag. |

ANDRES

| Let me take you to the sick bay, Franz. You should drink some brandy with powder in it and get rid of your fever. | Franz, du kommst ins Lazareth. Du musst Schnaps trinken und Pulver drin, das tödt' das Fieber. |

WOZZECK

| Yes, Andres, when the carpenter collects his wood shavings, no one knows whose head will lie on them. | Ja, Andres, wenn der Schreiner die Hobelspäne sammelt, da weiss niemand, wer seinen Kopf darauf legen wird. |

Scene Two. *Forest path by a pool. It is dusk. Marie enters with Wozzeck from right.*

MARIE

| The town is still quite far. Here's the way. Let's hurry. | Dort links geht's in die Stadt. 's ist noch weit. Komm schneller. |

WOZZECK

| You must stay awhile, Marie. Come, sit, here. | Du sollst dableiben, Marie. Komm, setz' Dich. |

MARIE

| But it's getting late. | Aber ich muss fort. |

WOZZECK

| Come. | Komm. |

They sit down.

| So far you've travelled, Marie. But never more shall your poor feet hurt you. It's quiet here in the darkness. Tell me, Marie, how long has it been since I first met you? | Bist weit gegangen, Marie. Sollst Dir die [12] Füsse nicht mehr wund laufen. 's ist still hier! Und so dunkel. Weisst noch, Marie, wie lang es jetzt ist, dass wir uns kennen? |

MARIE

| At Whitsun, three years. | Zu Pfingsten drei Jahre. |

WOZZECK

| And how long, how long will it still go on? | Und was meinst, wie lang es noch dauern wird? |

MARIE

jumping up

| I must go. | Ich muss fort. |

104

Frightened, Marie? But you are good! | Fürchst Dich, Marie? Und bist doch tromm?

laughing

And kind! And true! | Und gut! Und treu!

He pulls her down again on the seat. He bends over her in deadly earnest.

[Are you frightened?] Ah, how your lips are sweet to touch, Marie! | [Fürchst dich?] Was Du für süsse Lippen hast, Marie!

He kisses her.

All heaven I would give and eternal bliss, if I could always kiss you. But no, I cannot! You shiver? | Den Himmel gäb' ich drum und die Seligkeit, wenn ich Dich noch oft so küssen dürft. Aber ich darf nicht! Was zitterst?

MARIE

The night dew falls. | Der Nachttau fällt.

WOZZECK

whispering to himself

When cold, we don't shiver! You'll freeze no more in the morning dew. [But what about me! It has to be!] | Wer kalt ist, den friert nicht mehr! Dich wird beim Morgentau nicht frieren. [Aber mich! Ach! es muss sein!]

MARIE

What are you saying? | Was sagst Du da?

WOZZECK

Nothing. | Nix.

Long silence. The moon rises.

MARIE

How the moon rises red! | Wie der Mond rot aufgeht!

WOZZECK

Like blood-red steel! | [12] Wie ein blutig Eisen!

He draws a knife.

MARIE

You're shivering [like that?]! | Was zitterst [so]?

She jumps up.

What now? | Was willst?

WOZZECK

No one, Marie! If not me, no one! | Ich nicht, Marie! Und kein Andrer auch nicht!

Wozzeck seizes her and plunges the knife into her throat.

MARIE

Help! | [4, 7, 9, 10] Hülfe!

Marie sinks down. Wozzeck bends over her. Marie dies.

[5]

WOZZECK

Dead! [Dead! Murderer! Murderer!] | [6] Tot! [Todt! Mörder! Mörder!]

He rises to his feet anxiously and then rushes silently away.

Curtain.

Change of Scene. The curtain rises again fast.

Scene Three. *A low tavern, badly lit. Night. Apprentices and girls, amongst them Margret, are dancing a wild 'quick Polka'. Wozzeck is seated at one of the tables.*

WOZZECK

Dance, all you; dance away, leap, sweat and reek, for some day soon he'll fetch you, the Devil!

Tanzt Alle; tanzt nur zu, springt, schwitzt und stinkt, es holt Euch doch noch einmal der Teufel!

He dashes down a glass of wine, shouting down the pianist.

Three riders came riding up to the Rhine,
and went to my hostess to taste of her wine.
My wine is good, my beer is clear, my daughter dear lies on her . . .

[6] Es ritten drei Reiter wohl an den Rhein,
Bei einer Frau Wirtin da kehrten sie ein.
Mein Wein ist gut, mein Bier ist klar,
Mein Töchterlein liegt auf der . . .

He stops.

Be damned!

[7] Verdammt!

He jumps up.[1]

Come, Margret!

Komm, Margret!

He dances a few steps with Margret, then suddenly stops.

Come, let's sit down, Margret!

Komm setz Dich her, Margret!

He leads her to his table, and pulls her onto his lap.

Margret, you're hot as fire . . .

Margret, Du bist so heiss . . .

He presses her to him, then lets her go.

But wait till you're cold also! Can't you sing, girl?

Wart nur, wirst auch kalt werden! Kannst nicht singen?

MARGRET

To Swabia I will not go,
and nice long dresses I'll not wear,
for nice long dresses, pointed shoes,
do not belong to servant girls.

In's Schwabenland, da mag ich nit,
Und lange Kleider trag ich nit,
Denn lange Kleider, spitze Schuh,
Die kommen keiner Dienstmagd zu.

WOZZECK
flaring up

No! Wear no shoes, for one can barefooted go to hell fire!

Nein! keine Schuh, man kann auch blossfüssig in die Höll' geh'n!

singing

[For shame, my love, that wasn't nice!

[O pfui mein Schatz, das war nicht fein!

I'll not sleep with you at any price!]

Behalt den Thaler und schlaf allein!]

I want to wrestle, wrestle.

[9] Ich möcht heut raufen, raufen.

---

1. Büchner's Käthe becomes Berg's Margret. This is the original text:

WOZZECK
jumping up

Hey, Käthe!

He, Käthe![1]

He dances with her.

Come and sit down!

Komm, setz dich!

He guides her to his table.

I'm hot, hot!

Ich hab heiss, heiss!

taking off his coat

That's how it is! The devil takes some and lets the others go. You're hot, Käthe! Just wait, you too will be cold one day! Why don't you sing something?

S'ist einmal so! Der Teufel holt die Einen und lässt die Andern laufen. Käthe, du bist heiss! Wart nur, wirst auch noch kalt werden! Kannst nicht singen?

106

But what is that, there, on your hand?   Aber was hast Du [da] an der Hand?

WOZZECK

Me? Me?   Ich? Ich?

MARGRET

Red! Blood!   Rot! Blut!

WOZZECK

Blood? Blood?   Blut? Blut?

People gather round Margret and Wozzeck.

MARGRET

Surely blood.   Freilich Blut.

WOZZECK

I think I must have cut it, sometime on   Ich glaub', ich hab' mich geschnitten, da
my right hand.   an der rechten Hand.

MARGRET
imitating Wozzeck's tone of voice

How comes it then on your elbow?   Wie kommts denn zum Ellenbogen?

WOZZECK

I've wiped my hand on it there.   Ich habs daran[1] abgewischt.
jumping up

APPRENTICES

His right elbow wiped with his right   Mit der rechten Hand am rechten Arm?
hand?

MARGRET

Eh! Eh! It smells of human blood!   Puh! Puh! da stinkt's nach Menschenblut!

WOZZECK

What's that mean? That's my affair? Am   Was wollt Ihr? Was geht's Euch an? Bin
I a murderer?   ich ein Mörder?

YOUNG WOMEN

Surely it smells of human blood!   Freilich da stinkt's nach Menschenblut!

APPRENTICES

Blood, blood, blood, of human blood!   Blut, Blut, Blut, da stinkt's nach
                                                 Menschenblut!

WOZZECK

[What are you staring at?] Off! Or else   [Was gafft Ihr?] Platz! oder es geht wer
someone pays the Devil!   zum Teufel!

He rushes out.
The curtain falls quickly.

Change of scene.

Scene Four. *Forest path by the pool. Moonlit night as before. Wozzeck staggers on hastily, then stops*
as he searches for something.

WOZZECK
spoken

Where is it? Where can the knife be?   [12] Das Messer? Wo ist das Messer? Ich
Somewhere here, I left it somewhere,   habs da gelassen. Näher, noch näher.

---

1. added by Berg.

here somewhere — I'm scared. There!   Mir graut's. Da regt sich was.
Something moved.

whispering loudly

Still!   Still!

spoken

All is still and dead.   Alles still und tot.

shouting

Murder! Murder!!   Mörder! Mörder!!

whispering

Ah! Who cried?   Ha! da ruft's.

spoken

No. Only me.   Nein. Ich selbst.

Still searching, he staggers forward a few more steps and comes upon the corpse.

Marie! Marie! What is that so like a   Marie! Marie! Was hast du für eine rote
crimson cord round your neck? And was   Schnur um den Hals? Hast Dir das rote
that crimson necklace a gift, like the   [9] Halsband verdient, wie die Ohr-Ringlein,
gold earrings, the price of sin? Why is   mit Deiner Sünde! Was hängen Dir die
your fine black hair so wild on your   schwarzen Haare so wild?! Mörder!
face?! Murder! Murder!! They'll soon be   Mörder!! Sie werden nach mir suchen.
coming for me. That knife will betray   Das Messer verrät mich!
me!

He seeks feverishly for it.

Ah, it's here! [There are people! I must   Da, da ist's! [Leute! — fort!]
go!]

at the pool

Down! To the bottom!   So! da hinunter!

He throws the knife in.

It sinks through deep, dark water like a   Es taucht ins dunkle Wasser wie ein
stone.   Stein.

The moon comes up blood-red through the clouds. Wozzeck looks up.

See how the moon betrays me. The   Aber der Mond verrät mich. Der Mond
moon is bloody. Must then the whole   ist blutig. Will denn die ganze Welt es
wide world be shouting it? That knife   [12] ausplaudern?! Das Messer, es liegt zu
there too near the shore. They'll find it   weit vorn, sie findens beim Baden oder
when bathing, maybe when they are   wenn sie nach Muscheln tauchen.
mussel gathering.

He wades into the pool.
with some voice

It's gone now.   Ich find's nicht.

spoken

I ought to wash my body. I am bloody.   Aber ich muss mich waschen. Ich bin
Here's a spot and here something.   blutig. Da ein Fleck und noch einer.

lamenting

Woe! Woe! I wash myself with blood.   Weh! Weh! Ich wasche mich mit Blut.
The water is blood . . . Blood . . .   Das Wasser ist Blut . . . Blut . . .

He drowns.
¹ *The Doctor enters. The Captain follows the Doctor.*

CAPTAIN

Stop!   Halt!

DOCTOR
standing still

Do you hear? There!   Hören Sie? Dort!

CAPTAIN

Heavens! What a sound.   Jesus! Das war ein Ton.

He stands still.

---

1. Büchner introduces two anonymous citizens, not the Captain and the Doctor, for this
scene, who use the familiar 'du' for 'sie' throughout.

DOCTOR
pointing to the pool

Yes, over there!	Ja, dort!

CAPTAIN

It is the water. The water is calling out. No one has drowned here for a long time. Come, Doctor! It is not good to hear.	Es ist das Wasser im Teich. Das Wasser ruft. Es ist schon lange niemand ertrunken. Kommen Sie, Doktor! Es ist nicht gut zu hören.

He tries to drag the Doctor away.

DOCTOR
standing still and listening

Groaning like a man dying. [Hans!] Someone's drowning!	Das stöhnt, als stürbe ein Mensch. [Hans!] Da ertrinkt Jemand!

CAPTAIN

Eerie! The moon red, the mist grey. Do you hear? Again that sound.	Unheimlich! Der Mond rot, und die Nebel grau. Hören Sie? jetzt wieder das Ächzen.

DOCTOR

But softer. Now nothing.	Stiller, jetzt ganz still.

CAPTAIN

Come! Come quickly.	Kommen Sie! Kommen Sie schnell.

He drags the Doctor off with him. The Doctor quickly follows the Captain.

Change of scene [8, 1, 9, 2, 11]

Scene Five (Final Scene). *In front of Marie's house. Bright morning, sunshine. Marie's boy is riding a hobby-horse. Children are playing and shouting.*

CHILDREN

Ring-a-ring-a-roses, all fall down! Ring-a-ring-a-roses, all . . .	[5] Ringel, Ringel, Rosenkranz, Ringelreih'n! Ringel, Ringel, Rosenkranz, Rin . . .

They stop, as other children come rushing in.

ONE OF THE CHILDREN
spoken

Hey, you, Käthe! D'you know about Marie?	Du, Käthe! Die Marie . . .

SECOND CHILD

What is it?	Was is?

FIRST CHILD

Don't you know? They've all gone out there.	Weisst' es nit? Sie sind schon Alle 'naus.

THIRD CHILD
to Marie's boy

Hey, you! Your mother is dead	[7] Du! Dein Mutter ist tot!

MARIE'S BOY
still riding his horse

Hop, hop! Hop, hop! Hop, hop!	Hopp, hopp! Hopp, hopp! Hopp, hopp!

SECOND CHILD

Where is she?	Wo is sie denn?

Out there on the path, by the water. Draus liegt sie, am Weg, neben dem Teich.

THIRD CHILD

Let's go and look! Kommt, anschaun!

All the children run off.

MARIE'S BOY
riding

Hop, hop! Hop, hop! Hop, hop! [6] Hopp, hopp! Hopp, hopp! Hopp, hopp!

Noticing that he is alone, he hesitates a moment, then rides off after the other children.

Empty stage. The *curtain falls. End of opera.*
[11]

The last scene is not in the libretto.

Dissecting room. *Surgeon. Doctor. Judge.*

JUDGE

A good murder, a genuine murder, a beautiful murder, as beautiful as you could possibly ask for. We've not had such a beautiful murder in a long time.

Ein guter Mord, ein ächter Mord, ein schöner Mord, so schön, als man ihn nur verlangen kann. Wir haben schon lange keinen so schönen gehabt.

DOCTOR

— — — — — —

Discography / *David Nice*

Conductor	*Böhm*	*Boulez*	*Dohnanyi*	*Abbado*
Orchestra/Opera House	**Deutsche Oper, Berlin**	**Paris Opera**	**Vienna Philharmonic, Vienna State Opera**	**Vienna Philharmonic, Vienna State Opera**
Date	*1964*	*1965*	*1980*	*1989*
Wozzeck	Fischer-Dieskau	Berry	Waechter	Grundheber
Marie	Lear	I. Strauss	Silja	Behrens
Doctor	Kohn	Dönch	Malta	Haugland
Andres	Wunderlich	van Vrooman	Laubenthal	Langridge
Drum Major	Melchert	Uhl	Winkler	Raffeiner
Captain	Stolze	Weikenmeier	Zednik	Zednik
CD number	—	(CBS) CD79251 (2)	(Decca) 417 348-2DH2 (2)	(DG) 423 587-2GH2 (2)
Tape number	—	—	—	—
LP number	(DG) 413 804-1GG2 (2)	—	—	(DG) 423 587-1GH2 (2)

Bibliography

Of the numerous books in many languages about the opera, Volume One of George Perle's *The Operas of Alban Berg* (University of California Press, Berkeley, 1980) is the best background study and dramatic analysis, illustrated and with structural and musical examples. Douglas Jarman's *Wozzeck* in the Cambridge Opera Handbook series (1989) offers many source documents in English for the first time, notably Franzos' appreciation of Büchner, public correspondence around the first performance and Berg's 1927 'word about *Wozzeck*' and his 1929 lecture about the opera, *L'Avant-Scène* 36 was devoted to the opera in 1981, and includes a fine gallery of production photographs.

There are several English editions of the play, as mentioned in Kenneth Segar's article, of which the Methuen paperback *The Complete Plays of Büchner* (ed. Michael Patterson, 1987) contains a version by John Mackendrick. *The Drama of Revolt* by M.B. Benn (CUP, 1976) is the classic introduction to the theatre of Büchner.

Contributors

Mark DeVoto is Professor of Music at Tufts University, and the editor of the critical edition of the *Altenberg Songs*.

Kenneth Segar is a Lecturer in German at the University of Oxford, and a Fellow of St Edmund Hall.

Theo Hirsbrunner is a freelance writer on music and has published books about Boulez, Messiaen, Ravel, Stravinsky and Debussy.

Stewart Spencer is a freelance translator and co-editor with Barry Millington of *The Selected Letters of Richard Wagner* (London, 1987).

David Nice is a freelance journalist and broadcaster.

Jennifer Batchelor is writing a book on opera and film.

Acknowledgements

Grateful thanks are due to Elisabeth Knessl of the Archives of Universal Edition, Vienna, for help with picture research.

Errata and Extra Notes

page 54 Two sets of themes have been wrongly numbered, except for the initial appearances of themes [9] and [10] on page 77.

'Seduction Music' should be theme [10].
'Fight Music' should be theme [9].
'Wozzeck' should be theme [13].
'Knife' should be theme [12].

pages 64, 79 for [1] read [11]

page 85 for [11] read [13]

page 92 footnote 3:

This line ('Das Weib ist heiss! ist heiss! heiss!') is actually by Büchner, restored in the 1920 Witkowski edition of the play. In 1920, after Berg had been working from the Franzos/Landau edition for six years, Witkowski published an edition which for the first time linked the play to the historical events and character of Johann Christian Woyzeck, and restored the spelling of the protagonist's name. Berg did temporarily alter the spelling of his title page accordingly, but changed it back, and did not alter what he had already completed to bring it into line with Witkowski's text. Only in Act Three, scene two, on which we know from a letter to his wife he was still working in June 1921, did he follow Witkowski in certain points. He conflated Andres and the anonymous soldier of Franzos' text, and followed Witkowski's text for the song, 'O Tochter', where Franzos had 'other lads' singing of her escapade with 'die Schiffsleut'' not 'die Fuhrknecht'.

page 99 for *Launßau* read *Landau*

page 100 footnote 1:

Berg replaced Marie's story in the Franzos edition with the start of the Old Woman's tale (from the scene which he otherwise omitted). Franzos had adapted his text from a tale that Büchner intended the Idiot to speak in the same scene:

Once upon a time there was a King. The King had a golden crown and a Queen and a little baby boy. And what did they all eat? – They ate liver-sausage.

Es war einmal ein König. Der Herr König hatt' eine golden Kron und einen Frau Königin und ein klein Büblein. Und was assen sie alle? – Sie assen alle Leberwürst.

page 109 for [11] read [13]

Following Pages

Set model designs by Stefanos Lazaridis for the 1990 ENO production of *Wozzeck* by David Pountney at the London Coliseum. This was the first production of the opera by ENO and was conducted by Mark Elder, with Donald Maxwell and Kristine Ciesinski as Wozzeck and Marie. Act One, Wozzeck shaves the Captain; Wozzeck and Andres in open country; Act Two, Marie's room, the tavern, the barracks; Act Three, the Captain and the Doctor by the pond. (photos: Clive Barda)

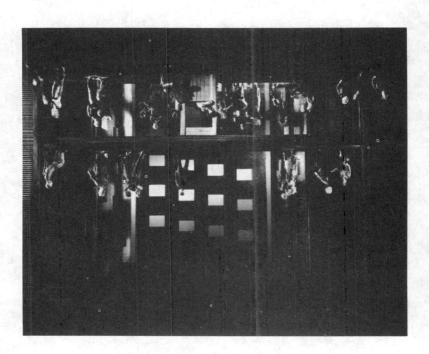